Cain's Crime

Cain's Crime

*The Proliferation of Weapons
and the Targeting of Civilians
in Contemporary War*

Thomas Trzyna

CASCADE *Books* • Eugene, Oregon

CAIN'S CRIME
The Proliferation of Weapons and the Targeting of Civilians in Contemporary War

Copyright © 2018 Thomas Trzyna. All rights reserved. Except for brief quotations in critical publications or reviews, no part of this book may be reproduced in any manner without prior written permission from the publisher. Write: Permissions, Wipf and Stock Publishers, 199 W. 8th Ave., Suite 3, Eugene, OR 97401.

Cascade Books
An Imprint of Wipf and Stock Publishers
199 W. 8th Ave., Suite 3
Eugene, OR 97401

www.wipfandstock.com

PAPERBACK ISBN: 978-1-5326-3246-4
HARDCOVER ISBN: 978-1-5326-3248-8
EBOOK ISBN: 978-1-5326-3247-1

Cataloguing-in-Publication data:

Names: Trzyna, Thomas N., 1946–, author.

Title: Cain's crime : the proliferation of weapons and the targeting of civilians in contemporary war / Thomas Trzyna.

Description: Eugene, OR : Cascade Books, 2018 | Includes bibliographical references and index.

Identifiers: ISBN 978-1-5326-3246-4 (paperback) | ISBN 978-1-5326-3248-8 (hardcover) | ISBN 978-1-5326-3247-1 (ebook)

Subjects: LCSH: Arms race. | Arms control. | War—Religious aspects—Christianity. | Combatants and noncombatants (International law). | Just war doctrine.

Classification: U22 .T79 2018 (paperback) | U22 .T79 (ebook)

Manufactured in the U.S.A.   05/25/18

For Hannah, Oliver, Benjamin and Grace.
May they thrive in a safer world.

Contents

Introduction | 1

1 The Incalculable Value of Human Life | 8
2 A Tragedy of the Commons | 22
3 Unwinnable Wars | 28
4 Dragon's Teeth | 51
5 Economic Imbalance and the Weapons Trade | 65
6 Just War? The Failure of International Treaties | 74
7 Targeting Civilians | 86
8 Our Better Angels? | 100
9 Conclusion: Cain's Crime | 109

Bibliography | 115

Introduction

A book about the proliferation of weapons and the targeting of civilians in contemporary war needs a foundation, an ethical foundation. The argument presented here is based on the work of a once-famous ethicist whose work deserves more attention: Joseph Popper-Lynkeus, an Austrian scientist, inventor, and philosopher whose work was prized by theorists as diverse as Albert Einstein, Sigmund Freud, and Karl Popper. Once a foundation is laid, it will be possible to survey the state of violence in the contemporary world and to ask whether concerted efforts toward the control of weapons, small and large, are possible, and if such efforts are realistic when so many of the leading nations of the world have economic and political systems that depend in significant measure on the invention, production, marketing, sales, and free dissemination of weapons.

Human lives have infinite value. That is, each human life has infinite value because it embodies a fully unique perspective on the cosmos that will appear once and just once in the history of the universe. While the same claim can be made for other lives, and especially other conscious lives, and while the claim may appear to be hyperbolic, please bear with it for a time. Every human life has infinite value.

Sadly, a case needs to be made for such an absolute ethical claim.

We live in a time when politicians speak freely about making the Syrian desert "glow," as did Texas Senator Ted Cruz during the 2016 US Presidential Primary elections. Did he mean glow from nuclear weapons, or from fire, or merely from intensive bombing, perhaps with incendiary bombs? Still worse, as reported by CNN and CNBC on August 3, 2016, Republican presidential candidate Donald Trump during a briefing asked three times what was wrong with using nuclear weapons. The Moroccan army has in fact made the desert glow in Algeria, where the UN High Commission for Refugees runs the largest current refugee camp in the world.

These refugees have fled the "state" of the Sahrawi Arab Republic, otherwise known as Western Morocco. There the Moroccan army has dropped napalm and white phosphorus on the UN camp to burn some of those refugees alive. The territory of the "nation" itself has been divided in half by an enormous earthen berm surrounded by land mines. We hear talk about killing the families of combatants, and going to war against major portions of the Earth's population. In December 2016, the citizens of Aleppo were being slaughtered as Syrian army forces retook rebel areas. It is terrifying to contemplate that the future US president would apparently consider using nuclear weapons as part of "ordinary" warfare, perhaps against targets such as ISIS in the Middle East.

At the same time, we face many "tragedies of the commons," crises that put the sustainability of life on this planet at risk. Global warming receives attention; so does major pollution of the air and water. However, the planet is also poisoned through the manufacture and sales of so many weapons that they are easily acquired and put into action to kill and to maim. The focus of this book is the proliferation of weapons and the sale of weapons by major powers that present themselves to the world as purveyors of peace.

There are more wars active on the planet than any assemblage of armies could resolve, even if more violence were capable of bringing an end to cycles of violence that are often hundreds if not thousands of years old, such as the ongoing conflict between Shia and Sunni Muslims, which is part of a longer conflict between the Arab and Persian civilizations. It is not an idle claim that the collective armies of the world do not have the resources to end the collective wars of the world. It is obvious after over a decade of war in Iraq and Afghanistan that the military forces of the United States are not sufficient to pacify or reconstruct those nations, whatever pacify might mean, unless the United States were to make a far greater commitment of men and material than it is willing to do. Even then, any "victory" would only spawn more conflicts. Given the volatility of the surrounding areas and competition with Russia and other powers, it is hard to imagine what total and complete victory could mean, short of engaging in another world war. In other areas of the world, the landmasses are so great and the availability of airfields, fuel depots, and other necessities so limited that it is difficult to conceive of successful military interventions in longstanding ethnic and national conflicts. Africa is the largest continent. The various wars in the Congo, Mali, Nigeria, Algeria, Western Sahara, and so many other places involve spaces that utterly dwarf the size of Europe.

Introduction

The manufacture and sale of weapons endanger us not only because weapons become available for killing and destruction of property. The purchase of weapons also twists the economies of nations by drawing resources away from infrastructure, education, and public services that contribute to the development of stable political and social systems. A deep cynicism underlies the manufacture and sales of weapons, as well. Nations that claim to support freedom rely heavily on selling—or in some cases giving away—weapons to less developed and less free nations. American foreign aid, for example, is often in the form of weapons that come from US manufacturers, with the bill paid by Congress, or from current stockpiles of weapons maintained by the Pentagon. Moreover, weapons are sold with the tacit provision that the merchant nations will always maintain a military advantage by keeping the latest and best weapons to themselves, though the major Western and Eastern powers that lead the arms race have not been able to keep some of the most sophisticated weapons out of the hands of powers they fear. Nuclear weapons have spread unpredictably.

Not only are there countless weapons available in the world and a staggering number of current wars, it is also true that contemporary wars are marked by the deliberate targeting of civilians. Just war theory, which is seldom applied except in debates after conflicts, aims to limit the damage of wars and to protect those who are not carrying arms. Yet economic and battlefield realities encourage strategists to kill civilians in order to end wars. The greater the suffering in a target nation, the more likely a state will fail or surrender, or there will be public uprisings to overthrow governments. Moreover, studies of so-called "collateral damage" tend to play games with the facts. Collateral damage cannot be limited to what can be measured immediately: the number of civilians killed in a drone strike or the number of children and hospital patients dead because of the short-term elimination of medical facilities and water-treatment systems. Collateral damage must be measured over the long term, because the damage tends to go on for a generation or more.

In the terms of familiar ethical theories that are consequentialist or utilitarian, a moral choice is weighed by its effects. On the classic utilitarian view, the question is whether an action benefits the greater number. (Utilitarianism, therefore, can be used to justify human slavery, if the slave owners are happy and larger in number.) Consequentialism, more generally, asks what are the measurable effects of an action. But how are effects to be calculated and over what period of time? Public discussions of wars often attempt to paint rosier outcomes by refusing to count many kinds of short- and long-term effects, notably those that affect noncombatants who are not outright killed by drones, bombs or crossfire. Long-term effects tend to be disregarded entirely. The reconstructions of Germany and Japan after World War II, with major international investment, represent outliers in successful recovery. Typically, nations that endure major wars are impoverished and unstable for generations, which is why one war or civil war in a nation is likely to be followed by another.

International treaties have attempted to limit all these effects of war, but those treaties are vague and have been limited in their application. The question that must be faced, therefore, is whether it is fair to assert the following: If an international political, economic, and manufacturing system has the effect of producing perpetual war, is it fair to call that system *designed* to produce that effect? Furthermore, is the problem of weapons as great a "tragedy of the commons" as global warming? Or, to put the query another way, is it fair to maintain that the effect—or even the design—of the arms-production system of the world is to produce the endless state of war and civil war that we experience? The effect of burning carbon fuel is to produce global warming. Whether anyone meant to increase storms or to increase sea levels or to make portions of the world uninhabitable is beside the point. The effect is a tragedy of the commons. Neither is it relevant to argue that weapons do not fire themselves, that the problem is bad people not bad weapons. Just as individual criminals will escalate violence by making use of whatever are the most lethal weapons they can acquire, so state and non-state political actors will turn to weapons because they are there.

This volume does not attempt to propose a solution to these problems. The solution has already been proposed by the United Nations and by other groups. Something must be done to decrease the availability of weapons. Above all, something must be done to make the manufacture and sale of weapons less attractive as an economic enterprise. States must come to understand the real costs of building significant portions of their economies on weapons manufacturing and trade. This book presents case histories and poses questions about points at which alternative choices were and are possible, choices that would not and that will not produce such disasters as the ongoing World War of Africa, which has led to the deaths of five million people, and counting, since 1960. This book provides evidence for its assertions. What is advocated here is an absolute ethical principle that asserts the infinite value of human lives. What is argued is that the evidence

Introduction

indicates that collectively, the population of the Earth, and above all the populations of the most prosperous nations, have created a world economic system that depends on the development, marketing, and sale of weapons and the promotion of continuous war.

The problem of access to weapons within the United States is obviously an aspect of the issue addressed here. However, the focus of this book is not on the National Rifle Association, the Brady Campaign to Prevent Gun Violence, the Second Amendment to the United States Constitution, or the horrific amount of slaughter taking place within the United States as a consequence of mass murders and other shootings. (The Second Amendment is the part of the Bill of Rights that has been interpreted to allow American citizens to own weapons, including assault rifles. The Brady Campaign was started by a victim of a near-presidential assassination.) The focus here is on the larger context, which includes the role of the United States as the premiere builder and marketer of weapons to the entire world, and on the weapons manufacturing and sales carried out by other leading nations, including many of the members of the United Nations Security Council, whose job it is to prevent violence worldwide.

Democracy, as a form of government through dialogue and deliberation, is fundamentally a commitment to pacifist governance or at the very least to systematically peaceful governance. Pacifism is the ideal state. This book does not argue for absolute pacifism. That subject and the religious ethics of pacifism are outside the scope of this inquiry. However, in the language of ethical theory, just as one can have a non-absolutist ethical commitment to the value of human life, one can have a non-absolutist ethical commitment to pacifism, to peaceful conflict resolution. To put this point less formally, a non-absolutist ethical commitment to pacifism means that a person aims to do no harm, but accepts the possibility that some extreme circumstances may arise where harming others is a moral necessity. The important debate, of course, is over what those circumstances may be. However, when nations build large portions of their economies around the manufacture and sales of weapons, when they are controlled to some degree by what President Eisenhower called the military-industrial complex, then those nations have ceased to make a prior and basic commitment to seek peace. It follows logically that to the extent that discussions of peace and the possibility of peaceful problem-solving are discouraged because of a national bias in favor of immediate military solutions, those nations have ceased to be full democracies. That is, those nations have made such a strong prior commitment to the use of violence, and to profiting from the use of violence, that their commitment to dialogue, deliberation, and peaceful resolution of conflicts has been badly skewed toward a quick resort to force. Governments whose economies are heavily driven by the arms industry have ceased to be both pacific in intent and fully democratic, because a dominant commitment to violent solutions reduces the likelihood that leaders will rely first and foremost on other, nonviolent, deliberative forms of conflict resolution. Evidence for this fact can be found in the fact that the United States Congress has not formally voted to go to war, as required by the Constitution, for nearly a century. Instead, presidents have taken the nation to war and then asked for legislation to support the required funding. Therefore the problem addressed by this book is not merely the problem of the human commitment to violence, it is also the directly related problem of the weakening of democratic forms of governance.

Internationally, the erosion of democracy can be seen most saliently in the process by which the Secretary General of the United Nations is chosen. The UN Charter provides that the Security Council will recommend a candidate to the General Assembly. However, that process of choosing and recommending candidates is secret. As of July 21, 2016, the President of the Assembly, Mogens Lykketoft, wrote all Permanent Representatives to protest the fact that the Security Council had carried out initial straw polls without revealing any details about the votes or the finalists to the President or to the General Assembly. Later in this book, the death of US Secretary General Dag Hammarskjöld will be reviewed as part of an assessment of the World War of Africa. That case, still under investigation, suggests that when members of the Security Council, and others, are dissatisfied with a Secretary General, they are prepared to use lethal violence to change the leadership. Where is democracy then?

Throughout, the arguments presented here are supported by data and by numbers. Those numbers include actual and estimated body counts, lengths of wars, numbers of weapons, percentages of national budgets, and other statistics. Data are necessary to make the case. At the same time, data can be numbing. Data can even obscure the main points. As a species we design devices to kill each other. We make money by creating, building and selling killing machines. National economies depend for their survival or health on income from selling and making weapons. Legislators depend on gifts from weapons companies to win elections. Legislators often take jobs from lobbying organizations and weapons companies when they leave

Introduction

office. Democracies are therefore warped by incentives to maintain and to support the weapons industry. We live by and profit by Cain's crime. We die by Cain's crime. If we are to survive, we must stop following Cain's path.

The United Nations has called for limits on weapons. In addition to that solution, this book poses a simple question: can the world create more genuine participatory government that is deliberative, data-driven, and democratic?

We are in a new age of reading. This book includes a bibliography and provides citations for direct quotations. It does not document every detail with footnotes. There are three reasons for this choice. First, the point is to advocate a position, not to provide exhaustive primary research. Second, data on numbers of weapons, wars, and deaths change constantly. Third, we live in a time when it is both possible and imperative to read with regular access to the internet. As you read, please do your own research and make choices for action.

1

The Incalculable Value of Human Life

Human life is infinitely valuable. A single human life is infinitely valuable, or at a minimum incalculably valuable. These statements may prove difficult to defend, and yet they are worth exploring in a planetary environment in which human lives are easily discounted or considered valueless. This inquiry runs the risk of becoming mawkish or sentimental, and yet because there are so many voices and forces that imply or state that human lives have no value, it is important to make this effort, particularly at a time when national leaders speak casually about killing large numbers of people who are different from them in race or religious affiliation. It is important to make a case that there is something uniquely valuable about every single human existence.

In 2016, the Black Lives Matter movement raised public awareness of the extent to which the news and the courts overlook the deaths of black American citizens who are killed in street violence and often by police forces. Over one hundred African Americans died at the hands of police in 2015. The toll in 2016 was better publicized and was rising rapidly. There was once hope that the nation had entered a place of post-racial peace. While the idea of a "post-racial" Obama period was fanciful, in the sense that centuries of racism and racist enculturation do not instantly disappear, the fact that Americans could speak about such a possibility at all indicated, for a brief moment, a hope that the United States had actually taken a definitive if not final step toward addressing and even eradicating racism. The continuation of mass incarceration of African Americans and the continuing killing of African Americans in the streets show that those hopes were wrong. African Americans constitute about 11% of the American population but upwards of 40% of the American prison population. White activists have responded to the Black Lives Matter movement with the claim that all lives matter. Of course all lives matter. The fact, however, is that African American people have been targeted for too long and their deaths have not in fact raised much concern, compared to the concern often expressed for the lives of others. Neither has mass incarceration raised much concern in the United States until recently.

This is part of a wider and well-known phenomenon one can see in any disaster headline. A plane goes down, and an American newspaper focuses on the fact that three Americans were on board. A French paper notes the three French on board. People tend to care more about those who look like them. Kohlberg's moral development theory tells us as much. Most people, most of the time, focus on those who are just like them, and therefore their ideas about what is moral tend to be applied only to people who look like them. The deaths of one hundred wedding guests in a Pakistani village erroneously targeted by a hellfire missile fired from a drone do not matter much in most of the world press. Those innocent victims can always be reclassified as suspected or potential enemies. Or they can simply be forgotten as insignificant. Racism is a fact of our existence. The deaths of close to 500,000 in the ongoing war for independence in Papua-New Guinea hardly merits a column in a paper.

What general principle can be invoked to make the case that every single life truly matters, infinitely matters?

Human lives have been destroyed in great numbers through wars, holocausts and pogroms, through civil violence and by many other means. We are accustomed to discounting the loss of life. It is worth repeating a familiar example for the sake of emphasis. A jihadist is killed by a drone strike, though upwards of 100 "innocent" civilians die in the same attack. Perhaps those additional dead were co-conspirators, or fellow travelers, or implicated in some other way. Perhaps they were merely part of the unimportant others whose lives do not matter, unimportant others who often speak languages that are not widely known, or whose dress or forms of government differ significantly from those dominant in much of the world. Once people are dead on the ground, they have no ability to explain that they were wedding guests, not members of a terrorist cell. Upwards of half a million people died in Iraq because of the destruction of infrastructure;

those are sad losses. Still, one can rationalize, because no one can guarantee noncombatant immunity when target nations are incapable of restoring basic services in a timely manner. Police use fatal violence to subdue an African American man wielding a butter knife, as happened recently in Seattle, or to kill a Native American carving a stick with his pocket knife, as happened recently in Seattle. Each of us develops a mental program to dismiss such events. The man with the butter knife was black and mentally ill. The Native American had an alcohol problem. These defects of health can be taken as reasons why they deserved to die, or at least why they were more deserving of death than people who are white and without any obvious mental impairment. For the second time in about five decades, the Seattle Police Department is under federal review because of racial profiling and excessive use of force. In another American city, on July 20, 2016, a black social-service worker, lying on his back with his arms in the air, was shot while explaining to police that the man next to him was autistic, did not have a gun, and was holding a toy truck. The police officer later said that he did not know why he had shot the black therapist.

At the turn of the twentieth century, the once-popular German-Jewish philosopher Joseph Popper (known by his pseudonym Lynkeus and often referred to as Joseph Popper-Lynkeus) published a short book titled *The Individual and the Value of Human Life*. Freud acknowledged that Popper had scooped his theory of dreams. Einstein was impressed by his ideas. The political philosopher and philosopher of science Karl Popper was honored to be considered a possible relation. Popper-Lynkeus's work is difficult to find now, especially outside the original German. (Popper-Lynkeus will be referred to as Popper, from now on, except when there is reason to distinguish him from his better-known peer Karl Raimund Popper, the political philosopher and philosopher of science.) Popper advanced a radical proposition in the form of a moral absolute. To understand just what he attempted, it will be necessary to say a few words along the way about different kinds of ethical theories.

Popper's short book is a defense of the following proposition, as translated into English by the late American professor of philosophy Joram Graf Haber:

> The obliteration of any individual who has not willfully or forcibly endangered another, even if that individual is thought to be "insignificant," is a much more important event than all the political, religious, and national events, and all scientific, artistic,

and technical progress of all centuries and people taken together. Whoever thinks this is an exaggeration should imagine that he himself or someone he loves is that obliterated individual and he will immediately understand this principle. (Haber, xiii)

Assuredly, in some respects this is an absolute moral principle that has so many large holes in it that one could drive a truck through it. The conditions set on the principle are amazingly broad. Anyone who has driven a car to the market has in some sense willfully and forcibly endangered others, because hydrocarbon pollution is carcinogenic and carbon pollution increases global warming with potentially catastrophic and irreversible effects. Any well-educated person knows these facts. Therefore, to choose to drive a car to the market rather than walking is a crime on Popper's view.

This objection to Popper's principle raises a matter that will be important later in this book: the differences among primary, secondary, and tertiary effects of actions. If I drive to the store with the intention of getting groceries efficiently, I probably do not mean deliberately to harm anyone. However, the pollution I create can have lasting deleterious effects on the health of people in my local area, a secondary effect. More broadly, a tertiary effect of my drive to the store is my car's and my own contribution to atmospheric carbon, which may lead to the rise of the sea and the deaths of people in low-lying islands or coastal areas.

The principle, as Popper states it, also leaves little room for redemption. Once I have committed such an act, I am in the category of those who have endangered others. Nothing can remove me from that category, and from that point on my life is one of those that can more acceptably be obliterated.

However, there is a kernel to Popper's proposal that deserves more attention and respect. Like the ethical theorist John Rawls, Popper argued that every human being deserves a minimum standard of living, because each life is valuable. It is Rawls who proposed the "invisible veil" test for ethical principles. On this theory, you can choose any ethical system you want, so long as you agree to live under it with the understanding that when you are born into this world you cannot choose your race, ethnicity, gender, intelligence, family wealth, state of health or disability, or other factors of your existence. Rawls' ethical theory can be viewed as an expansion of the principle that you should do unto others as you would have them act toward you.

In another passage, Popper suggests that in the case of a dire famine, when it may be impossible for everyone to live, it would be appropriate to cast lots to choose babies who would die so that others may survive. There is a hint of a rationale here for assigning higher value to some lives. This may or may not have been Popper's intention. However, it can be argued that newborns barely have self-awareness, and they have not accumulated perceptions, judgments, and thoughts about the world, humanity and the state of the cosmos. What makes an individual life valuable, perhaps, is the unique set of perceptions, ideas, and experiences that an individual possesses, a unique perspective on the universe. Alternatively, of course, one could argue that human potential is the key to our value, and hence the life of a baby should be worth more, say, than the life of an older person who is not productive. And Popper may have been thinking of another rationale entirely: that those who have lived longer have a network of connections.

Popper's argument can of course be extended to support the positions of the ethicist Peter Singer. Many species of animals have perceptions, emotions, memories, tool-making abilities, abilities to form hypotheses, and so forth. The purpose of this book is not to advocate vegetarianism or to explore the many ways in which humans behave savagely toward farm animals, though such positions might well follow from Popper's principle.

Whatever Popper's complete rationale might have been if he had worked it out more fully, he presents his principle as a "self-evident truth" by proposing the test that anyone ask whether he or she would be willing to be sacrificed, or to sacrifice a loved one, for any work of art or scientific discovery, or the totality of art and science. Popper allows that some people might indeed choose to make such a sacrifice; however, he objects that no one should ever be forced to make such a sacrifice. No one should be conscripted into an army, to use one of his examples. No parent should be forced to kill a child so that some principle, say Einstein's basic relativity equation, should be saved. After all, someone else might eventually rediscover Einstein's theory of relativity. No one, on the other hand, can remake a human life.

Popper's moral absolutism naturally calls for comparison with Kant's idea of a categorical imperative, and Popper's principle is open to the same kinds of objections that are made to Kant. Kant, for example, argued that if it is wrong to lie, it is wrong to lie at all times and in all circumstances. A typical objection to Kant is to imagine a situation where a good Austrian couple is housing a Jewish family in their basement during World War II.

The Incalculable Value of Human Life

The Gestapo come to the door and ask if there are Jews in the house. Should the head of the household tell the truth, or should the head of the household compromise his or her ethical principle? Kant's point is that once one compromises on an absolute principle, everything becomes relative. A person who lies once for a good reason is a person who may lie again, and hence that person's word is fatally compromised. Many people, however, affirm what is called a "weak absolutist" position: absolutes that hold except in extraordinary situations. The fact that the Austrian householder lies to the Gestapo does not totally compromise his or her truthfulness. That particular lie was, on balance, morally justified. In Popper's case, while he asserts his principle as an absolute, he allows that individuals have the right to sacrifice themselves for a work of art or an idea. They do not, however, have the right to sacrifice others.

The virtue of Popper's moral absolute is that it points out the circularity and the self-contradiction of arguments that call for the sacrifice of human life. If human life has value, then it is contradictory to call for the obliteration of human lives in order to save human lives. Moreover, if human life itself is the ultimate value, then it becomes difficult to argue that human lives should be sacrificed for abstractions or ideals such as "democracy" or "freedom" or "national honor" or any similar notion, much less for a formula or for a painting.

Popper admired many individual Christians and charitable Christian groups, but he disdained Christianity as a system for at least two reasons. One was the tendency of Christian belief to focus not on present existence, on human life as it is, but rather on some hypothetical future existence to which this life should be sacrificed. For Popper, the abstract idea of another world was not a sufficient rationale to sacrifice anything in this life. Second, like Bertrand Russell, Popper rued the long history of Christian violence against other Christians and against people of other faiths or no faith. The same reasoning could be applied with equal justice to Islam and to other religious and cultural traditions. Consequently, Popper rejects religious foundations for ethics, asserting instead his statement that life has absolute value.

Whether one is inclined or not to accept Popper's principle, what he calls his "motto," his thinking helps to mark a line between absolutist and consequentialist moral thinking. On a consequentialist view, one asks what the outcome is if one takes an action. If I sacrifice this individual in a medical experiment with the certain knowledge that the sacrifice will be the last experiment necessary to find the cure to all cancers, then does not the outcome justify the action? One will die so that millions may live. A key difficulty with consequentialist perspectives is the problem of limiting the time over which an action is judged. While it may be true, for example, that sacrificing this person today will lead to a cure for all cancers, it may also be true that sacrificing a duck or a worm tomorrow will provide the same research data. Alternatively, it may be true that sacrificing this person today will encourage a culture of human experimentation that will lead over fifty years to a holocaust. In any case, the "good" sought by utilitarian or other consequentialist ethical systems is some kind of absolute calculated at some particular moment in time. So one is back to defining some absolute measure.

An additional argument is commonly used to support consequentialist moral reasoning. The idea may be slightly abstract, though we encounter it on a daily basis. There is a lack of symmetry in arguments that one must make an absolute sacrifice now, because there is nothing absolute about the time frame in which one is asked to make the sacrifice. In other words, the moral choice is presented as an absolute, though the time in which the moral choice is to be made is not absolute. In public rhetoric, the "solution" to this dilemma is to argue that this particular moment is in fact an absolute. This is the last chance to buy a product; the last election in which it is possible to vote for freedom; the End Times of Christianity when there will be no more days for non-believers to convert. We live under constant pressure to believe that our particular moment of being alive is the last moment possible to make a difference. Indeed, there may be times when the danger is so grave that there is some truth to that proposition. But for the most part we are delusional if we think either that we are the end of history or the only people capable of making a positive difference.

In favor of Popper's principle, one can cite any number of instances in which an appeal to the value of a human life is made on the basis of self-evidence. These instances include emotional appeals, though it is not clear what the difference is between something labeled an "emotional" appeal and an appeal to a self-evidentiary nature. Aristotle's notion of a virtue, and G. E. Moore's notion of a moral sentiment are broadly relevant here. When we ask what actually drives moral decisions, the answer might be a utilitarian calculation, though it is more likely to involve reliance on patterns of ethical behavior (virtues) or on a moral "sense" that underlies those patterns. Television campaigns for donations to Amnesty International, St.

Jude's hospital, Operation Smile, and homeless centers feature photographs either of children or of feeble older people. The implicit argument of these advertisements, their appeal to moral sentiment, is that there is enormous value in these lives, so much value that everyone must work together to assure both their survival and a sufficient standard of living and freedom from deformity or disease. Is it appropriate or ethical to be cynical in the face of such appeals, or do those appeals in fact constitute a self-evident claim for the value of each human life? If the claim is not self-evident, then by what clear and well-defined standards do we make judgments about the comparative or relative value of human lives? The force of these pleas for support suggests that in fact they do have moral power, legitimate moral power. Moreover, the power of this kind of call to conscience or empathy lies in an aspect of human experience that may be prior to critical reasoning. In other words, the kind of moral theory that one needs to invoke to explain this kind of call to conscience depends upon something like moral feeling, moral intuition, or a sense of basic virtues rather than upon the kinds of mental calculation that is invoked by utilitarian ethical theories.

The whole enterprise of situational ethics and cases such as the famous trolley problem show that there are no universally accepted moral standards. In any case, our public spaces are full of precisely the kind of argument that Popper advocates: the intuitive judgment that every life is so valuable that efforts must be made to preserve that life and to guarantee that person a good level of health and opportunity.

While Popper may not have considered the idea of unique perceptions of the cosmos as part of his case for the value of individual, unique human lives, one can offer evidence for that kind of case, as well. Ishi, the last of the Yahi Native-American tribe whose life and death as a museum exhibit was chronicled by Theodora Kroeber, is a good example. Ishi's entire tribe was slaughtered by white immigrant families in north-central California in the latter half of the nineteenth century. He, his mother, and his sister were the last survivors, and for over a decade they lived in hiding in the canyons and brush of the buttes. For years after the deaths of his mother and sister, he lived alone, until he was so hungry he walked into "civilization." He was discovered naked and shivering in a slaughterhouse yard in Oroville, California in 1913. When he was taken, finally, to the University of California San Francisco anthropological museum for study, he recorded some twenty-plus hours of wax cylinders of myths and stories he had memorized as a child. He was the last speaker of his language and the last person to carry in his mind a set of stories about the relationships among animals, plants, and peoples that formed the religion, philosophy, and every other science of his now-extinct people. Yes, most civilizations will disappear, and all of us die eventually. However, is it plausible to maintain that nothing of value is lost when a people, a language, and an entire cosmology disappear from the earth? If not, is it not possible to argue that each human person's unique perspective on reality has equal and unique value? In this case, the anthropologist who "collected" Ishi and housed him in a museum for the balance of his life is instructive. Alfred Kroeber apparently fell into a deep depression after Ishi's death. The famous linguist Edward Sapir steadily worked Ishi for linguistic data as Ishi died, raising questions about whether his life had a lower priority than the data he could provide. Obviously, to Sapir and other linguists and anthropologists, what Ishi knew in fact represented a priceless cultural heritage. They failed, however, to pay adequate attention to Ishi the living person while they attempted to record for posterity what he knew of his massacred culture. Kroeber's wife Theodora did not publish her version of the story of Ishi until her husband died. Until the end, her husband was reluctant to discuss what had happened.

A similar instance is provided by the strange reality of the people who still live on North Sentinel Island in the Andaman Sea. If current accounts are correct, the North Sentinelese settled their small island during the eastward expansion of people out of Africa some 40,000 years ago, landing on the island by means of rafts. Since then, they have lived there in isolation, hostile to all comers. They have a reputation for being able to shoot an arrow accurately for 300 yards. A British expedition kidnapped a couple of Sentinelese in the late nineteenth century and took them to London, where they promptly died. The government of India, which currently controls North Sentinel Island, has decided that there will be a no-contact zone around the island to prevent any further deaths of fishermen who wander too close, as well as unwelcome interventions by those who may wish to explore the island and study its people. A single disease common to the rest of the world might erase the entire Sentinelese civilization. Ishi died of tuberculosis. There is an incalculable value in the continued existence of human persons who have lived out their own view of the world and the universe for the entire period since the late migration from Africa, who have during that time apparently known nothing at all of any historic, scientific, or artistic discovery or event of the rest of humanity, whether the emergence of Hinduism, Buddhism, Christianity, Islam; the various migrations and wars and empires; the scientific discoveries. The Sentinelese are not blank slates; they are slates differently scribed whose insights, though we may never know what they are, raise possibilities of alternative existences that are both encouraging and tantalizing. Their experience of what it means to be human, what it means to populate the planet Earth, must in some ways be radically different from that of any other people. They have, after all, managed to survive for 40,000 years without endangering their environment or invading the lands of others.

In a way, the existence of the Sentinelese people is a test case for part of Joseph Popper's thesis. At a minimum, he argues that human life is of incalculable or infinite value, value greater than all science, art, and history, because that value is self-evident, as tested by any human person's immediate assertion that the life of a loved one, or even of a complete stranger, is worth more than anything that has been thought or created. The Sentinelese are, so far as we have reason to believe, completely unaware of almost all human history and pre-history. They are unaware, so far as we know, of religions, empires, world wars, evolution, genetics, thermodynamics, calculus, artistic and literary movements, and whatever else has been accomplished by "civilized" peoples over the past 40,000 years. Yet their lives and their thoughts still have intrinsic value. Their system of values, whatever it may be, has after all allowed them to persist.

To turn to that other Popper, Karl Popper, the Sentinelese no doubt experience the three worlds that Popper hypothesized in his study of human consciousness and his study of the human brain, developed in collaboration with the Nobel laureate John Eccles. World 1 is our basic perception of what lies around us. World 2 is our emotional response to World 2 as well as certain instincts and patterns of behavior. World 3 is composed of our capacity to think, frame hypotheses, and test ideas. Higher animals such as primates have all of these abilities, including the ability to frame "theories of mind" and to hypothesize what other animal minds are thinking. Whatever theories of the cosmos the Sentinelese have developed, alone, during the last 40,000 years, the rich and unique content of the Sentinelese understanding of the world has incalculable value. In fact, whatever basic perceptions of the world and feelings about the world they possess are also valuable, because of the possibility that they have constructed for themselves a way of understanding reality that is different. The rest of us will probably never know what their view of life encompasses, though the possibility of such a different perspective on reality is an encouragement to consider whether we, too, might eventually construct an understanding of how to live that will be healthier than the one that currently dominates our world and our media. After all, while the websites about them speak as if they are "savages" and "hostile," they have managed, in their own way, to sustain a culture for 40,000 years without invading anyone else or damaging the planet.

Another way to consider this point is to reflect on what people now think about some of the major genocides of the past. While Popper may be right that we have a gut instinct to value human life when a direct appeal is made to us, we also tend to have an extraordinary ability to deny and to pay little attention to people who are not like ourselves. Do we distance ourselves from the reality of genocide and war? Do we rationalize? Do we engage in denial? How well publicized and protested were the following genocides *as they took place*? The Holocaust of the Jews and others during World War II? Mao-Tse Tung's Great Leap Forward? Stalin's purges? The Khmer Rouge genocide? The Bangladeshi war for independence? Or the war against women that will be discussed later? Rarely are genocides called out during their own immediate times. An exception, perhaps, is the extraordinary indictment of the Spanish conquest of the Caribbean penned by Bartolomé de las Casas, *An Account, much abbreviated, of the Destruction of the Indies,* based on his first-person witnessing of some of the events and their sequels. De las Casas' book demonstrates clearly that "savage" was a word better applied to the Spanish conquerors than to the natives of the Caribbean islands and Central America who were raped, tortured, murdered, and eliminated by the Spanish troops and the missionaries who came with them, as well as by the diseases they imported. The stories of Ishi and of the Caribbean natives are similar, though in some respects the fate of the Caribbean islanders was more cruel.

Bishop de las Casas wrote the following summary of his thesis in the introduction to his book. He had been a witness to many of the events he recorded.

> We hold as a thing most certain and true that in these forty years [since the discovery of the New World] there have been above twelve million souls—men, women, and children—killed tyrannically and unjustly, on account of the tyrannical actions and infernal works of Christians; and in truth I do believe, without thinking to deceive myself, that they were above fifteen million. (7)

The Incalculable Value of Human Life

Either one is prepared to accept the thesis that human life is incalculably valuable, or one rejects the idea or moderates it in some way. Whatever the case, any examination of the problem of killing, Cain's crime, needs to start with a clear understanding that life has intrinsic value.

A commitment to value human life, a commitment to turn to violence as an absolutely last resort, is a commitment to the principles of reason that underlie democratic forms of government. Democracy is fundamentally a pacifist approach to conflict. It is a commitment to solve problems by discussion, deliberation, and compromise. To turn toward violent solutions quickly, in the face of conflict, is to turn away from one's humanity. Popper's extreme principle can be taken to mean that anyone who makes a choice for violence has permanently forfeited his or her right to life. What are the implications of this view, extreme as it is? This question leads to one of the foci of this book: what is morally due to combatants and to noncombatants in war.

Just war theorist Michael Walzer has argued that those who work in weapons factories are no longer noncombatants and therefore no longer merit the protections that are theoretically supposed to be offered to noncombatants in war. One can of course disagree with Walzer's position. If his logic is based on the idea that those who participate in the economy of warfare are combatants, then noncombatant status should also be removed from anyone else who participates in any activity that is helpful to war. This in fact was the view of early just war theorists: that war was always a war between everyone in one nation and everyone in another nation, so that there were no noncombatants. What is the difference between someone who runs a lathe in a factory that makes bombs and someone who works in a bakery that supplies an army, or who grows wheat that is sold to the military? While this issue may seem impossible to resolve, in the sense that anyone who participates in a national economy is doing something to support any war effort, this discussion has a key role in the case presented in this book. Because when nations derive significant portions of their GNPs from the manufacture of weapons, those nations may put themselves—and their citizens—in the position of being perpetual combatants. The point is that one can be a combatant even when there is no war, because one's occupation is to prepare to be in war. So even if it may be wrong to call farmers combatants, because they raise crops that are used to feed soldiers, it may be correct to argue that when nations build significant portions of their economies around the production of weapons, a large number of people in those nations are perpetual combatants.

A nation that commits a major portion of its economy to weapons is also a nation that has turned away from the commitment to peace that is fundamental to democracy. To state this is no more than to restate President Eisenhower's concern that the American military-industrial complex has the power to warp the American national agenda. When an industrial complex of that kind has sufficient political and economic power, it can steamroll over voices that call for peaceful methods of conflict resolution. In such a nation, dialogue and deliberation are to greater or lesser extents replaced by a knee-jerk tendency to turn immediately to violent solutions and to waging wars.

According to two websites, Clearconnections.com and Siteselection.com, the number of people employed in the arms industry in the United States ranges from between 800,000, who are directly responsible for 10% of American manufacturing, and 3.5 million, a figure that includes those who manufacture, market, and maintain weapons. TheBlaze.com, in 2013, published a study that indicated 220,000 Americans were employed in the manufacture of small arms: pistols, rifles, shotguns, and the like. This number, the article noted, was about the level of employment at General Motors. For comparison, Bureau of Labor Statistics data for 2016 indicate that total construction employment in the US is about 6.6 million, which can be compared broadly to the estimate of 3.5 million involved in various aspects of the weapons trade. If the 3.5 million figure is a fair estimate of weapons employment for all kinds of weapons, that amounts to about 2.5% of total US employment in January 2016. For further comparison, the total size of the American military, according to GlobalFirePower.com, is about 2.5 million, including reserves. So there are about 6 million troops and weapons makers in the United States and about 6.6 million builders of homes, offices, and factories. Is this ironic? Do the numbers suggest a large enough commitment to war that the nation is not likely to be able to deliberate fairly about war and peace?

Is the United States still a full democracy if it dedicates such a large proportion of its resources to the invention, development, construction, sales, and proliferation of weapons that are used to fuel wars, terrorist assaults, and civil wars around the entire world? The economic aspects of this trade will be investigated later. Can one reasonably say that life matters, that all lives matter, in a world where so much energy and so many resources

The Incalculable Value of Human Life

are dedicated to ways to produce death? This question deserves serious attention. Of course, one can argue that there has never been a complete democracy or a fully functioning republic. Wealth and power of various kinds always confer greater power upon some individuals. The question asked here is whether the weapons industry, in particular, has had the power to skew democracies and the way that they make critical decisions about the use of national resources, the sacrifice of citizens' lives, their readiness to go to war, and the establishment of overall national priorities.

As a baseline for this inquiry, consider whether Joseph Popper's motto is correct: that any single human life is worth more than all that has been done in the arts and sciences over the course of human history. And consider his test: Which loved one would you sacrifice for, say, Einstein's theory of relativity?

2

A Tragedy of the Commons

A second aspect of Joseph Popper's principle is the notion that it is wrong "forcibly" or "willfully" to obliterate a life. In ethical theory, this raises the issue of primary and secondary effects, or what are often in ethical theory called "double effects." This book will entertain the notion that there are not merely double or secondary effects, but also significant tertiary effects of decisions that have moral implications. A weakness of many analyses of noncombatant casualties is that those analyses do not follow the long-term effects of wars and attacks.

Second Amendment activists in the United States commonly argue that guns are not the problem, rather criminals are the problem. American gun control advocates, on the contrary, cite evidence from other nations that when guns are well controlled, there is less violence, especially violence within families, suicidal violence, and other forms of violence that escalate because guns are readily available. From a Second Amendment advocate's perspective, the only problem is the primary purpose for the presence of a gun. If a gun is purchased for personal protection in the home, the owner of the gun should not be considered responsible if a housebreaker uses that gun to kill a family. The action of the housebreaker is a secondary effect, not a primary purpose. One does not prosecute a car manufacturer if a deranged person uses an automobile to kill a crowd of people. Neither should a gun owner be responsible if a deranged person steals a gun to commit a crime of violence. On this theory, the fact that a gun is designed to produce death or injury, while an automobile is designed primarily for transport, changes nothing in this assessment.

A Tragedy of the Commons

The debate over the relationship between gun ownership and violence within nations is complex because of the number of factors that can be considered. Crime Prevention Research Center, for example, makes a case that the evidence of a correlation between gun ownership and murder is not persuasive, though its essay "Comparing murder rates and gun ownership across countries," focuses on murder rather than other kinds of deaths caused by guns. Crime Prevention uses statistics to show that the United States is not as much of an outlier as some would argue, and that there are nations with worse murder rates. The Wikipedia site, "List of countries by firearms related death rate," on the other hand includes suicides, justifiable homicide, and accidental deaths, which has the effect of producing a different ranking of nations. Moreover, the nations with higher death rates than the United States tend to be unstable and the sites of recent civil wars or major civil discord. As stated earlier, it is not the purpose of this book to re-argue the Second Amendment debate. Most developed nations that have more gun control tend to have lower murder rates. The following figures give a taste of the issue: the annual gun death rate per 100,000 people for Mexico, where officially only one gun store exists, is 7.64; for the United Kingdom, where there are significant limits on gun ownership, the rate is 0.23; and for the United States, the rate is 10.54. Nations with far higher gun-death rates than the United States include Brazil, Colombia, Guatemala, El Salvador, Honduras, Jamaica, Swaziland, Uruguay, and Venezuela. Some of these nations have death-by-gun rates five and six times that of the United States. These figures leave out the numbers of people injured by gunfire in their homes or on the streets.

For the purposes of this book, there is value in considering that weapons are different from other manufactured products, because they are made for the purpose of injuring or killing. While an owner of a weapon may purchase that weapon for the primary purpose of defense, hoping never to use the weapon, once that weapon is present in a home or business, it makes secondary effects, secondary purposes possible. The problem of double effects has been exhaustively studied by ethicists. A person who maintains weapons for self-defense, for example, can claim not to be responsible for the fact that those weapons are used in a massacre. The original owner of the weapon had no intent that those weapons be used in such a way.

Yet in the case of weapons, there may be both secondary and tertiary effects for which the original purchaser should accept some level of responsibility. Weapons are like a long-lasting agricultural poison sprayed on an environment. A police officer in Uganda may carry a weapon for protection during his or her duties. Stolen, that weapon may be used (secondary effect) to kill. Sold to a tribe on the border that traditionally required men to steal a cow to win a wife, the weapon may be used to murder farmers in another village, where traditionally the required theft would be carried out with minimal violence. The use of guns in these transactions may lead—in fact has led in the case of the Karamojong people of Uganda—to a major change in the social structure, to the point that a once-aggressive people that maintained a culture of violent rites of passage and thefts for bride prices has now become a population engaged in frequent massacres using automatic weapons. This is a tertiary effect (Jabs, personal communication). Traditionally, a Karamojong adolescent would take a spear and go steal a cow from a neighboring village, perhaps a village of people who were members of a different tribe. The stolen cow could be used for a bride price. Now, Karamojong youths are more likely to take an automatic rifle, or several automatic rifles, and steal a herd of cattle while slaughtering many people who attempt to defend their herds. Villages find themselves in a state of perpetual war that has brought in national armies and rendered some areas of the countryside unsafe for any traveler. Guns used for primary defense are used secondarily for rites of passage, which leads to a tertiary use of those weapons for constant regional warfare. So long as ammunition is available, and more guns can be smuggled in, the warfare is likely to continue, and the social structure of the region will continue to be transformed. Older weapons will continue to be used, and the likelihood is that the economy of the area will change from herding to a culture of snatch and grab raids in which it becomes increasingly difficult for anyone to continue the traditional pastoral life. How different is the situation of the Karamojong from the social transformation that has taken place in some American ghettos where gangs now have access to automatic weapons? Fortunately, studies of gangs in the US and the UK indicate that urban gangs tend to target each other rather than uninvolved "civilians," though drive-by shootings sometimes injure or kill bystanders. Dystopian fiction may portray scenarios like the devolution of Karamojong culture, yet that kind of wider violence, while common in war and revolutions, seems not to be a part of urban gang life in the developed world. Mexico, however, presents a different and more complex version of the Karamojong story. Whole areas of Mexico are considered off-limits both to tourists and to local citizens. The drug war there among cartels and the government poses a danger to bystanders, and in that case it is not clear what definitions should be used. Is Mexico at war? Is it experiencing a form of revolution? Is the form of gang activity so extreme that it differs profoundly from gang life in the US and the UK, to cite two examples? Perhaps the situation in Mexico is more comparable to the political and gang violence in the Indian district of Jharkhand. The common element in all these forms of violence, however, is access to large number of weapons and to automatic weapons.

One fact is clear: whatever the primary purposes of many weapons in the world, their secondary and tertiary uses are part and parcel of social changes that include desensitizing populations to the incalculable value of human life.

Throughout the world, many inventions that have good primary effects or purposes have turned out to possess either deleterious or disastrous secondary and tertiary effects. Some of these effects have been studied for over a generation, and the ethical and political dialogue continues to be stuck with respect to the question: Who should bear the responsibility for those double and triple effects, and what should be done to mitigate those effects?

Roger Revelle's discovery of global warming due to carbon emissions is the best-known case of such secondary effects. While many treaties have been written and approved by many governments, there is still reluctance on the part of major nations to accept responsibility for global warming, as well as stark denial on the part of many political and religious leaders. The dangerous side effects of doping animal feed with antibiotics have been debated for over a generation, and yet antibiotics continue to be added to feed so that animals can be raised in crowded facilities, with the consequence that bacterial agents may develop immunity to every class of antibiotic. Sampling indicates that common pharmaceuticals can now be found in estuary and ocean water, where they are taken in by sea life that is caught for human consumption. Antidepressants, antibiotics, and hormones in birth control medications are among these medications.

These cases and many others, such as air pollution in China, are instances of tragedies of the commons. The commons are those goods we all possess and that we should all seek to protect: potable water, breathable air, agricultural and aquacultural areas free of poisons and medications, and of course global temperatures that are conducive to life and that do not bring about significant increases in storms and other disasters. Some areas of the Arabian Gulf, to cite another example, are now threatened with daily maximum temperatures that will soon make life outdoors impossible. Even now it is painful merely to watch construction workers labor in full sun in temperatures above 110 degrees and in humidity ranging over 90%. The 2015 heat wave in India killed 2,330 people by June.

It is fair to maintain that peace is another common possession, equal in value to other common treasures like fresh water and global temperatures that allow plant and animal life? Actions that make peace unlikely across the globe also constitute a tragedy of the commons. The proliferation of weapons that endanger peace constitute a tragedy of the commons. What all of these tragedies share is the same set of responses, which are often rationalizations, forms of denial, and special pleading. The fact that none of these goods has ever been perfectly available or available without problems of quality or distribution does not change their status as common goods: goods that we share; goods for which we must take responsibility; goods we must protect and preserve.

In the case of weapons, the special pleading and denial are so powerful in the United States that Congress has passed legislation prohibiting researchers from using federal money to research the effects of guns and gun ownership. Comparisons to other nations are easy enough to find; however, the researcher at the University of Washington Medical School and the Children's Hospital of Seattle, Dr. Frederick Rivara, who carried out basic demographic and statistical analyses of the dangers of guns in the US produced results so troubling that the National Rifle Association worked with like-minded members of Congress to put an end to that line of research.

Weapons are produced in enormous quantities with the stated purpose of protecting nations and individuals. Weapons must be produced continuously because each nation or police agency wishes to have weapons capable of defeating the best weapons possessed by potential aggressors. Older weapons are sold to poorer nations, or warehoused, or wholesaled. Above all, weapons flow over borders and enflame conflict. Only one shop sells weapons in Mexico. It is run by the federal government and is located in Mexico City. The weapons used by drug cartels in their wars with each other and the national authorities come from outside the country, hundreds of thousands of them each year from the United States, where they can be purchased freely and where American gun shops line the roads near the border. Journalist's Resource estimates that over 212,000 weapons enter Mexico from the US annually. Other resources (InSight Crime accessed

3/22/16) suggest as many as 2,000 weapons per day, which would amount to roughly 730,000 weapons per year. Mexico is not alone in this problem. A Canadian government report published in 2007 estimates that 48% of the guns used in crimes in Canada are smuggled from the United States and comments that this may be an underestimate. This is a tragedy of the commons.

3

Unwinnable Wars

How large is the problem of war at this time? Steven Pinker's recent book, *The Better Angels of Our Nature*, argues that we are living in one of the least violent periods of human history. Pinker's evidence and conclusions will be critiqued later in this book. Whether there has been a lessening of violence is debatable, in part because of the tendency of those who report the casualties of war to define those casualties to exclude noncombatants and people who die as the result of what can be called secondary or tertiary effects of wars. If a civilian dies in an explosion aimed at a combatant, she is a noncombatant. If a civilian dies a week or a month later because the local hospital has been destroyed, or the water supply is contaminated, most analysts do not consider that a noncombatant death. Those deaths must be counted, too. Yes, at some point one may begin to count people who died of natural causes or who would have died in any case for some reason. Many calculations of the excess deaths by war attempt to take into account normal death rates. To set the cut off almost immediately after an attack is surely to bias the count in a way that does not honestly represent the real totals of those who die as noncombatants or who die as "collateral damage."

In any case, returning to Pinker's thesis, whether violence has decreased is irrelevant if there is still a vast amount of formal warfare between and within nations, insurrections, epidemics of ethnic cleansing, and centuries-old if not millennia-old ongoing conflicts among religious and ethnic groups. If one begins with Joseph Popper's motto, one death is enough to matter, because that one life had an incalculable if not an infinite value. There is little satisfaction or purpose to be gained by pointing out that mass slaughter may be reduced compared to the times of Ghengis Khan. The problem of organized warfare and murder that currently exists needs to be measured in some way and then faced not only with respect to how large that violence is, but also with respect to how impossible many conflicts are to address, much less to resolve. Many ongoing wars are in places where there is limited infrastructure, vast spaces, and very small likelihood that any contemporary armed force, no matter how large and how well funded, could successfully contain those conflicts and then stay and maintain some semblance of peace, even for a short period.

The issues addressed in this book are broader than mere calculations of the numbers of dead, however liberal or circumscribed the criteria for attributing particular deaths to specific wars. As anyone can see by consulting the various databases available on the web and in other sources, deaths in war are often discounted if they are not the deaths of combatants, if they do not occur immediately, or if a larger war can be broken into multiple smaller wars that tend to diminish the scope of the damage. One of the examples developed at length later in this book is the so-called World War of Africa, which began with the independence of the Republic of the Congo in 1960, if not before. One can easily lose track of the enormity of this ongoing conflict, with its five million and counting dead, if that overall conflict is broken into its sub-parts and if one imagines that brief periods of truce or exhaustion constitute clear boundaries between separate wars. Those smaller wars or conflicts have names like the Simba Rebellion, the Ituri conflict, the Katangese Secession, the First and Second Congo Wars, the CIA operation against Che Guevara in the Congo and on the shores of Lake Tanganyika, the repeated outbursts of Hutu and Tutsi violence that crossed several international boundaries, the Lord's Army of Uganda and its incursions into the Congo, the genocidal war against the Baluba people, and many other conflicts that are in fact part of a single and nearly seamless, ongoing state of war and siege. Merely counting the dead is also not enough because that measurement does not begin to indicate the scope of damage to cultures, to family systems, to economic systems, and to the possibility that stable states can emerge and prosper out of the ruins.

President George W. Bush declared a war on "terror." When one considers war in the contemporary world, it is critical to include the effects of overall terror, that is, the condition of living in any state where there are large numbers of weapons and where people have been socialized to use them readily to address conflicts. Consequently, while the probably incomplete picture of international war presented here is based heavily on body counts reported in a variety of sources, in fact a true assessment of the situation ought to take into account smoldering wars and conflicts where the availability of weapons and patterns of oppression add a deadly dimension to daily life.

Terror can be understood well by drawing on the American experience, although the state of terror is no doubt far worse elsewhere. The point of *ruling* by terror is to use open violence in a way that is extreme, visible and relatively rare. Too much open violence will produce a reaction. Moreover, though citizens may wish to benefit from the terror that is inflicted on marginalized groups, those same citizens may not want to carry out or witness terror too frequently. Grisly deaths are unpleasant unless one is fearfully sadistic or totally desensitized. Moreover, too much terror damages normal economic activity because it can bring repercussions such as investigations, negative publicity, reduced trade, and a distaste among the public for shopping and for visiting public places. Therefore, for example, in a "well run" terrorist state lynching should be uncommon and strategic, not an everyday event. Further, it is best if those who are oppressed do much of the policing themselves. Richard Wright's autobiography *Black Boy* provides a perfect picture of how terror operates. As a small boy, he once drank out of a white drinking fountain in his Southern town and observed that the water did not taste different. His mother slapped him. Richard had to understand that there were lines one did not cross, because those who violated the norms were likely to be lynched. No white man or woman needed to discipline Richard; his mother was complicit in the system of terror. She administered the punishment, and by refusing to discuss the matter, she also indicated, powerfully, that the rules were so binding and terrible that they were never to be discussed. This is how rule by terror should operate: it is silent and it is enforced by its own victims.

This system of terror is still in operation, and though rule by terror does not require a large number of deaths, in the last year the number of African Americans shot to death in debatable circumstances exceeds one hundred. One cannot read the accounts of these deaths without contemplating their effect on communities of color in the United States. The message is that you had better watch out where you go and how you behave, because this could happen to you, too. A few well-publicized and gruesome deaths are sufficient to convey the message to tens of millions of people. The American situation of course became more charged in 2016 because of the inflammatory statements and promises of the future president, Donald Trump, who proposed to build a large wall to keep out Mexicans, implied that Mexicans who came to the United States were rapists, and also proposed to bar all Muslims from entering the United States while initiating surveillance of all mosques in America.

Claire Bernish reported recently that some US police departments are now in favor of legislation that would allow them to use drones both for surveillance and also for combat, a notion that brings back to mind the decision of the African American mayor of Philadelphia to drop an Air Force bomb, by helicopter, on the fortified house occupied by the radical movement MOVE. That 1985 bombing resulted not only in the deaths of MOVE members but also in the burning down of a large portion of the surrounding minority neighborhood. In these cases, the police and other authorities considered themselves to be at war with the citizens they were sworn to protect.

July 2016 opened another dimension of the militarization of American police departments. The African-American veteran of Afghanistan who killed five police officers in Dallas and wounded seven others was, after hours of negotiation, killed by a robot carrying a bomb. The newspapers on July 9, 2016, were full of stories about this case, with some of the elements of just war theory being invoked. One of the issues that was raised is the distinction between war and police work. The object of warfare, says the *Seattle Times*, is to kill people (July 10, 2016). That objective, of course, is open to question, since the object of war is often taken to be to win some concessions, or territory, or to reduce the will of the enemy to fight any longer. Setting aside that issue, the article suggests that the object of police work is to obtain justice. Police are not to be judge, jury, and executioner. If there is a reasonable way to starve out, or disable, a killer, then that method should be used. Sending in a bomb is a technique of total war that eliminates any possibility of a trial. Surely the robot could have been equipped with a camera to determine if the killer had a large bomb or some other apparatus that would have prevented the police from starving him out or using a sleep-inducing gas or tear gas. In any case, the killer was not given justice. Another question is obvious: Would police have used a robot bomb if the perpetrator had been white? Did the use of a bomb merely underline the fact that disproportionate force tends to be used against African Americans by police agencies? Is there a war within the United States against people of color?

Cain's Crime

A copy of the *Seattle Times* delivered to my home in June 2016 came wrapped in an advertisement for bulletproof backpacks and notebook covers. Parents were advised to purchase these to protect their children, as if owning a small piece of armor could guarantee protection against a mass killer in a school, as if children could be trained to position their armored backpacks or notebooks between a gun barrel and their bodies, as if a killer would cooperate by shooting where the child had positioned the tiny shield. The ad stated that the armor weighed no more than a liter of bottled water. That's 2.2 pounds. Add a bulletproof gym bag and notebook to the backpack, and the total extra weight of the armor would be a mere 6.6 pounds for a small child to lug and wield. This is madness, unless by some fluke the ad was meant to be satire.

As many American Civil Rights leaders pointed out repeatedly, violence is not measured solely in terms of deaths and injuries. It is measured by the state of mind that is created in those who are under a system of oppression in which they are often reminded of the penalties for disobedience, which include the near systematic failure to bring charges against police who may have broken rules, and the roughly 1% of the American population that is in jail, in detention, or on parole.

George W. Bush, of course, had a different kind of terror in mind when he declared the war on terror. The logic of that terror is a bit different from the logic of using terror to control a minority population. The fear today is that people without power who have enormous grievances will strike out randomly and without warning. Whereas there may have been a logical limitation to the number of lynchings in the United States, in terms of the number of people willing to participate in the crimes and the number of deaths needed to cow a population, some forms of terror on the current international scene are based on the notion that there is virtue in dying during a terror attack and a limitless need to punish the enemy civilization that is responsible for attacks on Islam. The common element in terror is the message that there are no noncombatants at all, that everyone in an enemy population is always at risk. To put the case bluntly, the "war on terror" and worldwide instances of racial and ethnic discrimination and "cleansing" suggest that we are in a state of total war.

How many conflicts are there in the world today? To what extent are those conflicts exacerbated by the availability of ordinary weapons, not weapons of mass destruction, but rather weapons that can be used to kill masses of people? How many conflicts are merely smoldering? The point of the following inventory is to show that there is more present conflict than can reasonably be "solved" by any application of military force by any nation, even if one were persuaded that war can bring an end to long-standing ethnic and religious conflicts. Further, the addition of more weapons to the present number of conflicts merely worsens the tragedy of the commons that we already face. The data presented in this chapter are not organized in an elegant fashion because there does not appear to be a rationale for organizing violence, as does Wikipedia, in terms of smaller wars and larger wars, or for listing deaths by continent or types of wars. In fact, a burden of the listing here is to challenge the ways that scholars work to circumscribe their accounting of violence in order to appear to be more precise and cautious in their claims, when what they are discussing and presenting is not about precision or caution at all.

Judith Gardam, who studies noncombatant casualties and the various international treaties and principles that have been written to try to limit war, cites a 1988 estimate that there were at that time three million casualties a year from twenty-five ongoing wars. She estimated that four fifths, 80%, of those deaths were civilians. Wikipedia maintains a heavily edited and documented "List of ongoing armed conflicts" that is bound by many specific criteria. Wikipedia maintains separate lists of ongoing armed conflicts and ongoing protests. The list of protests is extremely short and does not begin to include the large number of protest movements outside the Western world. The list of armed conflicts is circumscribed by criteria such as these: the combatants must be "organized armed groups," civilians must be "directly targeted," and there must be at least 100 deaths with at least one in the past year. Note that this definition is radically unsatisfactory. A civilian in the vicinity of a military strike, who is not directly targeted, does not count. What is direct targeting? Being in the area or being an intentional victim? The language allows for any number of interpretations. Do the over 100 African Americans killed by police in 2015 meet the standard for inclusion in the list? Probably not. Random deaths spread over an entire nation may not constitute a war even though those who belong to a targeted group may judge that they are victims of a war. Wikipedia's estimates of battlefield deaths for the last three years indicate only about 175,000 dead per year, a number that differs significantly from Gardam's figure. Which is more correct, three million a year or 175,000? These kinds of discrepancies and disagreements complicate any review of the data.

Anyone who lived through the American war in Vietnam will recall the famous Thursday evening news reports of the week's fatalities, according to which the US and its allies always killed two or three times as many enemy troops as they lost. In the political context of that war, it was important to show that more of them died than those of us. It was important as well to demonstrate that because we could kill more, we were stronger and likely to prevail. Now, anyone who dies after a drone strike may be counted as a possible belligerent. As Wikipedia states, "fatality totals may be underestimated or unavailable due to a lack of information." Fatality totals may also be overestimated for political purposes if the public is to be persuaded that their side is winning, in the same way that fatalities can be visually underestimated. And fatality totals may be underestimated to reduce public concern about the level of slaughter in distant war. In the United States, the public are not to see pictures of coffins arriving home so that the reality and immediacy of American and allied deaths can be hidden. Photographers are not allowed access to the air base where the bodies arrive from abroad. In the case of the American War in Vietnam, the still-emerging totals indicate that the Vietnamese suffered millions of deaths, to which can be added the illnesses and deaths of those still affected by Agent Orange: the cancer victims, the victims of birth defects, those who suffer from other diseases likely caused by chemical agents used during the war. So that those Thursday evening reports were accurate at least in the sense that the Vietnamese people died in far greater numbers than did American troops.

Wikipedia's recent tabulation of wars that fit the site's definition indicates that a minimum of 174,760 people died in 2015. For past years, the estimates can vary by a factor of 5. That is the level of uncertainty in the estimates. As an example of the difficulty of establishing accurate counts, consider the situation of the Muslim Rohingya minority in Myanmar, a group that may number between 1 million and 1.5 million. Of these, perhaps 450,000 or more have left Myanmar for refugee camps or exile since 1978. Wikipedia says 881 died in Myanmar in 2015, though this number may also include groups such as the Karen and other minorities that have been at war with the central government for decades. With 450,000 fleeing by sea and trekking into relatively hostile areas of India, under a thousand dying per year seems low. Amnesty International also says United Nations estimates are probably low, because there is some evidence that thousands of people have attempted to leave by sea in boats of marginal quality. People who disappear are difficult to count; they leave few bodies to be discovered.

Other sources indicate over 600 Rohingya deaths in refugee camps alone in 2015 (Victor).

Past massacres have presented the same problems of determining correct body counts. In May, 1980, citizens of Kwangju, South Korea rose in protest against the government. The government initially estimated 200 deaths; later figures suggest the number was around 2,000. In Mexico City in October, 1968, students rose against that government. Initial estimates of the number of people shot to death by the army ranged from thirty to 300. More recent estimates suggest the number of deaths was in the range of 3,000. In these and other cases, it matters who does the counting. These deaths in Kwangju and Mexico City, however, are generally not included in counts of deaths by war, because they are cases of civil war or of massacres of civilians by a country's own armed forces. Siyan Chen and Paul Collier's works on recovery from civil wars begin with a tally of forty-one civil wars that have taken place between 1960 and 2003. They state that there have been 125 civil wars since the end of World War II. Many authorities do not count deaths from civil conflicts.

Wikipedia's estimate of the deaths associated with the Donbass war in the Eastern Ukraine is probably wrong for a different reason. The Russian government declined to provide data on the deaths of Russian soldiers, probably in part because that government denied at times that Russian soldiers were involved. Research revealed, however, that Russia issued payments to some 2,000 widows, which increases the total estimated deaths from around 9,000 to 11,000 (Eremenko). In short, there is reason to believe that estimates of the number of deaths from wars should often be far higher. The estimates of the deaths in the cases of the Korean and Mexican uprisings were increased in part because of counts taken at graveyards a year later: how many families turned up to remember those who had been killed, and how that number of families differ from official government statements about the deaths.

Not all of these people are killed by firearms. Some die of starvation. Some die at sea by thirst or drowning. Some are mobbed, or killed with sticks and machetes and knives. Some, such as the refugees in South Sudan who hide in swamps, are killed by crocodiles, poisonous snakes, or other predators. While it would be impossible to prove the role of guns in these deaths on a case-by-case basis, it is fair to hypothesize that when people flee in large numbers, they are driven off not merely by mobs with clubs but more likely by groups that possess superior weapons, such as pistols, rifles, automatic weapons, armored vehicles, helicopters, bombers, and all the other paraphernalia of somewhat modern armed forces. Here as elsewhere in this book, it is true that it would be difficult to develop a case that would stand up in a court: that is to say, if proving a connection between the proliferation of weapons in the world and the continuing slaughter requires the identification of specific weapons, those who used the weapons, an assessment of motive and opportunity, and all the rest of the steps required by a good court, that would be as impossible as proving, say, the movement of this or that molecule of hydrocarbon from a gas station through a particular car taking a needless journey all to way to the formation of a specific carcinogen or to a molecule in the atmosphere that is responsible for some clearly defined cancer or some precisely calculated portion of the increasing warmth of the planet. The case must be built otherwise, out of broad collections of data. What then are the current wars, according to Wikipedia and its multiple editors and critics?

There are three general points to be made through an examination of such lists. First, the level of conflict is staggering, as are the numbers of deaths. Second, when one considers the locations of some of these conflicts, the size of the territories and the absence of modern infrastructure, it becomes plausible that many of these conflicts are unwinnable. Third, all of these conflicts have deep historical roots that will require something other than more violence or dreams of immediate resolution through the application of more force. No amount of force could be applied to resolve these conflicts over any realistic amount of time. The resolution must come peacefully. America's current wars in Afghanistan and Iraq are evidence enough of these problems.

The deadliest current wars are grounded in conflicts within Islam that have been enflamed by Western interventions. The division between Shiite and Sunni Muslims dates to the generation after Muhammad, when the community bypassed Muhammad's son-in-law and elected Abu Bakr to be the first Caliph, who directly followed Muhammad after his death in 632 CE. Sunni fundamentalism, the other important force in these conflicts, has arisen many times in the past centuries, including movements and uprisings in Saudi Arabia, Sudan, Egypt, India, Afghanistan, and elsewhere. These facts are well known, as are the names of many of the key leaders, such as Abu Wahab in Saudi Arabia at the end of the eighteenth century, the Mahdi in the Sudan at the end of the nineteenth century, Waliullah in India in the late nineteenth century, Said Qutb in Egypt, who founded the Muslim Brotherhood in Egypt in the mid-twentieth century, and more recent leaders of military and religious movements, such as the Salafists. These conflicts have been exacerbated by ethnic animosity between Persians (or Iranians) and Arabs.

At the same time, not all the violence in the contemporary world is due to conflict within Islam or between the West and Islam. There are many ethnic and racial conflicts in Africa, such as between Berber and Black African populations in West Africa, as well as between Black African populations, as in parts of Nigeria, Eritrea, Ethiopia, Somalia, the Democratic Republic of the Congo, and Cameroun. Still other conflicts may be emerging, as in the Uighur area of China. Behind many of these conflicts lie ongoing colonial or neocolonial projects to extract resources and to maintain control over important resources, as in the case of the Democratic Republic of Congo. There is also a simmering conflict between the Berber peoples of North Africa and Arab populations. Boualem Sansal's many books about conditions in his nation of Algeria in the twenty-first century offer a window into this problem, where Berbers are often told simply that they are Arabs and are discouraged from following their own historical traditions, which of course include the mighty Carthaginian Empire that fought Rome.

The catalog that continues here does not include any wars in South and Central American nations, though the economic situation in Venezuela is quite threatening, with citizens lining up at the nation's borders to be able to go to a neighboring nation to buy basic foodstuffs. Of course, an inventory of this kind taken a decade or two ago would have included large numbers of deaths in wars, civil wars, and police actions in Brazil, Chile, Peru, Argentina, Nicaragua, Colombia and other South and Central American nations, although once again the data bases that list wars often exclude the violence of armies against their own people or the violence of civil wars and uprisings.

For the sake of a running inventory of carnage, the Russian and American invasions of Afghanistan have produced upwards of two million dead since 1978. The American-instigated Iraq war has killed upwards of one million since 2003. The Syrian Civil War in five years has killed about half a million, and the various Boko Haram (Books are Forbidden) insurgencies across Central Africa have killed about 20,000. This is barely a beginning of the list, and already the difficulty with reading or presenting the data is that there are so many places at war that after a while the mind cannot keep track of the totality of the carnage and the various reasons that people have taken up weapons against one another.

Wikipedia maintains lists of wars organized according to how many people died in a particular year, with broad categories of numbers of deaths. That, too, is a mind-numbing way to contemplate the carnage. Wikipedia lists "Arab separatism in Khuzestan" in the category of conflicts that caused 100–999 deaths in the last year, for example, and says the conflict started in 1922. Khuzestan is an Arab section of Iran on the Euphrates River delta, and it was the focus of the 1980–88 trench war between Iraq and Iran, during which the United States provided Saddam Hussein with weapons. About half a million soldiers died in that conflict, as well as another half-million civilians. It seems unfair to separate current separatist activity from the major war that tore the area apart. In the case of this war as in the case of so many others, definitions of starting and stopping dates often seem arbitrary, although it is certainly possible to point to periods of intense warfare.

A group working to improve cancer care in Iran in a project associated with the Fred Hutchinson Cancer Research in Seattle were told that the chemical weapons used by Iraq in this Khuzestan conflict are likely responsible for the huge spike in cancers in this region and elsewhere in Iran, because Iranian troops were drawn from around the country and have often returned to their home regions. These victims, like the victims of cancer in Vietnam, are not counted in most inventories of casualties.

Conflict between Kurds and Turks since 1984 has produced over 45,000 deaths. Chaos in Somalia has killed half a million, including some people in neighboring Kenya. Warfare along the border of Afghanistan and Pakistan has added another 60,000 since 2004. The Mexican drug war has killed over 150,000. It is interesting to compare this total to the estimate of the number of American citizens killed inside the United States as a result of gang and other violence associated with the American effort to interdict narcotics. One estimate of that total from Narcosphere was 5,700 Americans dead, which was described as three times the number of American troops killed in Afghanistan by the same date, March 2012. Five thousand seven hundred dead in the US by 2012 and 150,000 dead in Mexico by 2016. Which nation suffers more from the American drug problem?

The new Libyan Civil War has taken about 14,000 lives with no end in sight. The crisis in Yemen has killed upwards of 11,000, though that war needs to be viewed in the context of the on-again, off-again division of the nation into north and south and even the war between Communist Yemeni rebels and the Sultanate of Oman forty years ago. Ongoing fighting in the Sinai has killed close to 3,000 recently. War continues in the area that broadly includes the western Sudan (the provinces of Kordofan and Darfur), Chad, southern Algeria, and other nearby areas. This conflict has roots in an ancient competition among Arabs, Berbers, and the peoples of Central Africa. The conflict has been exacerbated by the gradual desertification of northern Africa, which has strained the capacity of the region to provide food and water for its populations. The Darfur conflict has killed nearly 180,000 since 2003. The conflict in Darfur is an excellent example of an unwinnable war in the sense that the Sudanese province of Darfur is larger in territory than the entirety of Great Britain. What modern army, at what cost, would be capable of installing the necessary infrastructure and occupying such a distant, dry, and vast area for long enough to put down a longstanding guerilla war that has ethnic and climatic roots that reach back over 5,000 years? The desertification of the Sahara has been going on at least that long.

No sooner did South Sudan gain independence after a thirty-year war with Sudan than a civil war began that has killed over 50,000 since 2013 alone. The president and vice president of that nation, each representing one of the historically dominant Sudanese tribes, are at war with one another. The slow war between India and Pakistan in Kashmir has killed about 4,000 since 1948. The sporadic Marxist insurgency in North East India has killed 25,000 since 1963, including several hundred in 2015. The deadlock between Israel and the Palestinian territory has killed about 24,000 since 1964. Drug war in Colombia cost 220,000 dead, beginning in 1964. The Naxalite insurgency in India has killed nearly 14,000. Religious conflict in the Philippines has killed 44,000 since 1969. Religious rivalries in Pakistan account for another 5,000. Discord in the Uighur area of China has killed at least 900. These totals do not include recent wars that may be considered concluded, such as the Bangladeshi war for independence, which led to the deaths of approximately 3,000,000 people and the rape of upwards of 400,000 women. That war is not over, at least in the sense that war criminals are still being prosecuted, as they are of course in the cases of the Algerian war for independence and even for World War II.

In many of these instances, a few hundred deaths are evidence of grievances that go back generations. Since 1976, the Oromo people of Ethiopia, who consider themselves the majority, have fought against what they perceive to be the unfair dominance of the Amhara people. Up to 9,000 have died in this conflict since 1992. The border between Eritrea and Ethiopia continues to be a conflict zone, though the number of dead has decreased since the last full war ended in 2000, leaving up to 300,000 dead in a fight over a stretch of desert that the UN believes should be Eritrean, though Ethiopia continues to occupy it. Wikipedia does not note any deaths in Mauritania. There, the Berber population has traditionally dominated and even enslaved the Black African population, and according to Human Rights Watch, the Berber government of Mauritania has stripped citizenship from over 50,000 Black Mauritanians, chiefly people who held positions of influence, and has expelled them from the country. How many deaths are associated with those expulsions is anyone's guess. Landlocked Mali is plagued by a similar ethnic conflict, as are many regions of the Sahel. Similarly, the Ogaden insurgency continues sporadically in Ethiopia, with some 11,000 dead since 1995.

As noted earlier, the Democratic Republic of the Congo is the primary site of the World War of Africa, which Wikipedia currently parses as four separate conflicts: the Allied Democratic Forces insurgency; the Kivu conflict in the east, the Lord's Resistance Army conflict that extends into Uganda, South Sudan, and the Central African Republic; and the Ituri conflict. Together, since just the 90s, these conflicts account for nearly 1.8 million dead, and of course the roots of these wars run back to the fragmentation of the Congo after independence in 1960. Nearby, while the Angolan civil war is over, the Angolan exclave of Cabinda, up the coast, continues its independence struggle. Thirty thousand have died in that war for independence.

Sectarian conflict in Nigeria has killed over 16,000 since roughly the turn of the twenty-first century. This figure obviously does not include the one million dead during the Biafra War of 1967–70, when one province and tribal group attempted to secede from Nigeria. It is not clear whether the current estimate of 16,000 dead in the twenty-first century includes those who have died or been executed for protesting conditions in the oil-drilling areas of the Nigerian coast, though Wikipedia reports some 2,300 dead in conflict along the Niger River delta. The well-known Nigerian writer Ken Saro-Wiwa was executed with eight others by the Nigerian government for his activism representing the interests of his people against the depredations of Royal Dutch Shell in the region.

Unwinnable Wars

A small war smokes in the Algerian Maghreb. A few thousand have died recently, far fewer than the 250,000 who died during the "dirty" civil war that rent Algeria from 1991–97. Boualem Sansal, who was fired from his government post for writing fiction and essays about his native Algeria, paints a dire picture of life in the police state that Algeria has become. Along the Algerian border of Western Morocco, otherwise known as Sahrawi, there are as many as 165,000 refugees of the Sahrawi war of independence from Morocco. At times, Moroccan forces have bombed the camps with napalm and white phosphorus. The war for that empty, gravel-covered desert once known as Spanish Sahara was won by Morocco by means of building an earthen wall hundreds of miles long with bulldozers and then laying minefields. For many of the conflicts listed here, there are similar stories of refugee camps that persist for decades, sometimes under the direction of the UN High Commission for Refugees.

It is still difficult to travel in the Balkans; some borders are closed, other roads are dangerous because of roving bands of brigands or ethnic police. Russia continues to fight small wars in the Caucasus. The Kurds are fighting in Syria, Turkey, Iran and Iraq. A small insurgency continues in the southern end of Thailand. Since 1963 the western end of Papua-New Guinea has been the site of a liberation movement to free West Papua from Indonesia. Somewhere between 150,000 and 400,000 have died in this conflict, which seems to be nearly invisible in the Western press. Shining Path may have been defeated in Peru, but conflict continues, with over 70,000 dead since 1980. The killings since the 60s and 70s in Chile, Argentina, Guatemala, Nicaragua, Brazil, and elsewhere do not make the list, because these cases of state terrorism are over for the present: they are not producing any more countable deaths, though anthropologists and forensic researchers are digging up mass graves. The Nogorno-Karabakh conflict between Armenia and Azerbaijan continues to kill a few people, with a running total of nearly 30,000. In 2016 Azerbaijan began to call back students studying in foreign universities so that they could fulfill their military service, very likely in raids against Armenia. Small insurrections in Bangladesh and Tunisia round out Wikipedia's account, plus a tally of "spillover" deaths in Lebanon from the Syrian Civil War. Other places with several hundred deaths, places that may break out with much greater violence, include Egypt, Mali, Burundi, and of course any ISIL incursions into Turkey.

No doubt this list is far from complete. Honduras, for example, has had the highest murder rate in the world for some time. Why Mexico's war with its drug cartels figures in the Wikipedia survey while the same kind of war in Honduras does not is an open question. The press notices some conflicts and passes over others. Due to the difficulty of reaching some parts of the world, accounts will always be approximate. The press also likes to build up stories about conflicts, particularly stories that can be resolved within the twenty-four or seventy-two-hour news cycle. Any story of conflict that can be resolved that fast is almost by definition a story that will be "resolved" by violence, by the application of superior force and probably superior technology. That makes a good story, even a feel good story.

Shortly after the beginning of the ISIL insurgency, or the Islamic Caliphate, or Daech, or any of the other names by which it is called, a group of Yazidi Muslims, a small Shiite sect, found itself surrounded and threatened with death by starvation, thirst, or gunfire on a sacred mountain. The Yazidi faith combines elements of Zoroastrianism, Islam, and perhaps Christianity. Air power rushed in to save the isolated Yazidi and to provide food. American Special Forces landed on the mountain and discovered that, after all, the Yazidi there were not starving. Subsequently the Yazidi returned to Syria and Iraq, where apparently they were not so severely threatened, though over the following years stories of Yazidi women being raped by ISIS fighters appear often in the news. What are the facts? How is an outsider to evaluate these stories in a world where claims of rapes by Huns were part of World War I propaganda? What methods could be used to protect the Yazidi, other than short-term firefights? Shortly afterwards, a group of Iraqi Turkmen found themselves surrounded, and a force of Iraqi, Kurdish, and American troops rescued the Turkmen. The papers pointed out that the Americans were fighting in collaboration with several forces that have recently been their enemies and will likely continue to be their enemies. The newspapers do not explain how this series of crises began, or whose weapons are used on all sides, or what thought has been given to the consequences of forming constantly changing alliances of convenience to address crises that are a week in duration and often appear not to be such crises after all. American military and technological superiority feature in these narratives. While it is wrong to calculate the value of human lives in dollars, the amounts spent on weapons are meaningful. Money spent on war is a measure of the willingness of nations to fight; money spent on weapons is also a measure of what is lost to other national priorities. It costs about $18,000 an hour, averaged over a year, to keep an A-10 Warthog close support fighter jet in the air and about $42,000 an hour to keep an

F-15 flying. A single Hellfire missile costs $70,000, and sometimes more sophisticated missiles have been used to "take out" a single pickup truck with a couple of suspected enemy volunteers.

Depending on the lens one uses, and how small a portion of the story of the Yazidi or the Turkmen one sees, those stories can be read in the newspapers as heroic efforts to effect emergency rescues, or they can be read in ways that reveal a far more complex tale of intermittent persecution and safety that includes not only the sufferings of the Yazidi and Turkmen, but also the sufferings of the Sunni who were attacking them. These news reports can also be read cynically as Western media telling compelling stories or ramping up public desire for heroic military action that demonstrates the supreme power and precision of American forces. If I rely on the news media, all I have at my disposal for understanding this situation are fragments of information provided by reporters on the ground and by various governments. These sources rarely provide me with adequate context. What is one to believe in these news stories apart from the fact that they repeat the same basic narrative line, which is an urgent call for American intervention and more guns?

If I pull my lens back farther, I see a story in which the United States has supplied weapons to Saddam Hussein's army in a war against Iran that cost millions of lives. Earlier the United States was a staunch ally of the Shah of Iran, who had been put in power by Western states. The West supplied Iraq with some of the weapons it used to fight Iran, which was supplied by the West. In fact, the United States was Iran's largest weapons supplier until the Revolution of 1979. By that year, the US was selling as much as $4 billion annually in arms to Iran. The United States also supplied weapons to Afghan patriots fighting the Soviet Union as well as to the Iraqi Army that has recently lost them to the Sunni insurgency. Later, US forces fought the people America armed, including Saddam Hussein, the Taliban patriots who fought the Soviets, and elements of the ex-Iraqi army that have joined other coalitions. Not one of these conflicts has led to a political or social resolution. The military forces appear to have wasted their efforts, at least so far as longer-term peace is concerned.

Another way to examine the range of violence in the world is to look at putative cases of genocide. These are cases where the Bush Doctrine of Right To Respond appears to have its strongest traction. In such cases, the doctrine goes, one can shortcut the usual considerations of just war theory—not that those considerations receive much attention from governments—because the emergency is so obvious that there is no time for such niceties as negotiation. Clearly those in danger are cases of last resort. Plausibly, considerations such as noncombatant immunity or the choice of proportionate force may also be set aside, at least immediately.

Gregory Stanton's Genocide Watch issued its last report available online in 2012. His taxonomy lists levels of danger, the last being denial that anything happened, the preceding three being Polarization, Preparation, and Extermination. By the polarizing phase, those to be eliminated have been scorned, labeled, and often segregated. The 2012 report lists nine nations where active genocide is taking place: Democratic Republic of the Congo, Sudan, Syria, Somalia, Afghanistan, Pakistan, North Korea, Myanmar (formerly Burma), and Ethiopia. Stanton's criteria are somewhat broader than those applied by the Current Conflicts site, because he takes note not only of genocide against tribes of people (the Tutsi, for example) but also of categories such as the women and children targeted by the Lord's Army and the government officials targeted in Afghanistan, in addition to the usual kinds of political and religious targets, such as opposition parties, Muslims in some parts of the world and Christians in other areas, such as in Indonesia and in areas under the control of the new Caliphate. Another twelve nations are listed among those preparing for genocide, and twenty-six are considered to be in the polarization phase. That's a total of forty-seven nations out of 196 on the planet, or 24% of the world's countries that are at the higher stages of the genocide scale. Many other genocides seem to have run their course recently, such as those in Cambodia, Rwanda, Liberia, Sierra Leone, Angola, Mozambique, Bosnia, Sri Lanka, East Timor, and some ethnic conflicts in Micronesia.

North Korea presents a striking case. It is possible for a government to carry out genocide against its own people, as did Argentina not so long ago, and China, Russia, and Germany at other periods in the twentieth century. No doubt this list is incomplete. Depending on the estimates one consults, about a quarter of a million North Koreans are in concentration camps, prisons, and re-education camps where they are being tortured, starved, or worked to death. Much of the remaining population lives in conditions of near-starvation. Seoul is within quick striking distance of the demilitarized zone. The North Korean army is enormous, if perhaps poorly equipped. The country has nuclear weapons. If attacks on the Anuak of Ethiopia constitute genocide, as reported in some sites, or the displacement of several hundred thousand people in the Central African Republic or the eastern provinces of the Democratic Republic of the Congo qualify as genocide, then certainly the concentration camps of North Korea must count as genocide. And what of the elimination of white farms and tribal persecution short of genocide in Zimbabwe? (The Anuak are a Nilotic ethnic group of about 300,000 people who live in areas of Ethiopia close to South Sudan.)

If the Alawi or Alawites of Syria lose the current civil war, they may face genocide. The Alawi are a sect within Shia Islam that does not believe in worshipping in mosques and whose members hold that they are reincarnated five times before becoming stars in the heavens. Their theological views are anathema to Sunni extremists, as are the theologies of other Shiite groups that believe in messianic figures or reincarnation, or that blend Islam with aspects of earlier religious traditions. Are there still genocidal attacks on the remaining Baha'i or other religious minorities of Iran? Does the conflict between the Sunni government and Shiite population of Bahrain border on genocide? The situation in Mauritania has been noted already; some call it "the other Apartheid," and estimates range as high as half a million Africans exiled or in camps.

People from other parts of the world who visit the United States of America sometimes comment on what they perceive to be continuing genocide against Native Americans. The facts of seventeenth- through nineteenth-century genocide cannot be denied. Theodora Kroeber's story of Ishi, the last Yahi, offers good evidence for the totality of genocide in some cases. The creation of reservations, then the termination of tribes, and more recently actions by tribes themselves to de-list members continue a pattern of actions that is leading to the erasure of Native America.

With respect to the contribution of weapons to solving the world's problems, one way to pose the question is to ask whether it would be possible to create a truly neutral United Nations force that could put a stop to these genocides, and then perhaps move on to end the current set of wars? Perspective can be gained by reflecting that as of 2016 the United States spent more in Afghanistan, in current dollars, with no clear objective and no progress, than the US spent on the entire Marshall Plan after World War II. With all of its resources, it is not clear that the United States can afford either the cost in dollars, material, or personnel to carry out its recent wars in the Middle East.

Precisely how large would a neutral United Nations force need to be in order to address the complete list of genocidal or near-genocidal situations listed above? Even if that were a complete list, which is unlikely. And how much larger would such a force need to be to bring an end to the current wars, in addition to the current genocides and threatened genocides? Even if the United Nations were completely impartial in is operation and able to reach consensus, the force necessary to shut down current genocides and mass civilian displacements must exceed the resources of the major armies of the world, quite apart from what such an expenditure would mean to the social-service budgets of the nations involved: the damaging effect on education, health care, and infrastructure projects.

Of course, there are occasions when limited violence or the threat of violence is successful. If it were not, then we would not turn to it so routinely. Perhaps some strategic bombing around the Yazidi's sacred mountain in Iraq saved the lives of some Yazidi for a time. Yet is there any solution to this problem?

Yet there is still another major war that has been left out of consideration, because it must be considered a war, and perhaps the longest in human history, though it does not always use sophisticated weapons. This book is primarily about the danger posed by manufacturing and marketing weapons in such large quantities, and grounding significant portions of national economies in the manufacture of weapons, that wars with guns, tanks, fighter jets, bombers, drones, missiles, and other technology are a certainty. Perhaps the biggest war and longest war on Earth, however, does not depend so heavily on guns. That war began before guns were invented, and it is often carried out without weapons more complex than kitchen knives, pans of boiling oil, buckets of water, and hands. That war has a place in this book, however, because without considering it, one cannot begin to comprehend the scale of human violence and the underlying attitudes toward life, the underlying lack of value for life, that allow wars to flourish.

Nobel Prize winner Amartya Sen first pointed to the problem of the missing women of Asia, though slaughter of women is common in other areas as well, such as the killings of women documented to have been committed by the Lord's Army in Uganda and the pre-Islamic Bedouin tradition of killing female children. Since Amartya Sen's first estimates in 1990, there have been extensive debates about the phenomenon and the numbers. These estimates are based often on demographic data and birth rates. The estimates take into account what is known about practices in many cultures where it is easier to kill a bride than to return a dowry, where women are considered a liability rather than a productive asset, or where female babies may be aborted or killed at birth where they are a burden to families or where their existence does not allow families to guarantee male heirs as well as the continuation of traditions in which male children look after the elderly. Conservatively, this genocide totals some sixty million persons at any given time, a number that is calculated by using basic human birth rate statistics to compare the number of women who probably should be present in the world to those who are actually alive, based on census data. Census figures in some nations may be unreliable, of course.

A reasonable but less conservative estimate of the number of missing women at this time is 108,000,000 who have been killed. Working out the running total would produce a much higher number of missing and murdered women for any century, because this is a situation where that number of women continues to be missing, decade after decade, in proportion to the overall population of the world. Bongaarts and Guilmoto's estimate for 2035 is 150,000,000; the UN estimated 163,000,000 in Asia alone in 2005. All of these numbers are suspect in the sense that it would be helpful to have an estimate for the entire twentieth century, an estimate that could be compared to such figures as fifty million dead in World War II or thirty to forty million dead in Mao Tse Tung's Great Leap forward in the years around 1960, when many Chinese were forced to return to the country and where they died attempting to farm in times of a drought that led to famine. While the following strategy may be crude, suppose that one takes the 100,000,000 estimate as accurate for a time when the world population was 7 billion. That would work out to roughly one in every thirty-five women born being killed. Using that death rate and estimating by the three generations of the twentieth century, when the global population rose from 2 billion to 4 billion to 7 billion, one arrives at a total number of missing women for the twentieth century that is twice any one of the estimates for the current period. That's a range of between 130 million and nearly 330 million women killed and missing. Three hundred thirty million is approximately the current population of the United States of America. So the slaughter of women in the twentieth century may have equaled the current population of the United States. Moreover, it is not clear if a number like this should be understood to include the women killed in other wars, or whether this total is entirely additive: the women and female babies killed in cultures where women have low or no status. Surely this killing is genocide, too, and should be counted with the more limited though also important, meaningful, and terrible events, such as the annihilation of tribes who stand in the way of deforestation or who practice a different religion. To these missing women can be added the victims of human trafficking, most of them female, who total about 2.5 million each year. They may be alive; they may be dead. While it could be argued that these are not war crimes that are carried out by states or by revolutionary movements, what is the difference between governments looking the other way at bride-murder, or the actions of trafficking gangs, and organized movements that use guns to carry out genocide by raiding villages? The war against women is a feature of human culture.

Moreover, there is a qualitative difference between killing with guns, drones, and aircraft and the routine murder of unwanted female babies, wives, and daughters who disobey cultural norms. The killing of women and of female babies is more intimate than killing in war. A soldier who fires a missile, controls a drone, or shoots a rifle at a distance probably does not know his or her victim. A killer within a family knows the victim and is likely related to the victim in a way that is far more intimate, say, than the way that Hutu and Tutsi neighbors in Rwanda often knew the people they slashed to death. What links all of these killings, however, is cultural expectations of violence. So it is not possible, by mobilizing clever definitions of warfare or combatants or noncombatants, to separate the war on women from more traditional kinds of wars with guns between governments or between governments and liberation movements. This link is evident to some revolutionaries, though. The published principles of the Mexican Zapatista movement led by Sub-Commandante Marcos begin with a litany of assertions concerning the rights of women. Sub-Commandante Marcos apparently understood that the war on women lies at the root of other violence.

The number of wars, the types of wars and genocide, taking place now is staggering. As noted earlier, Steven Pinker's assertion that things are getting better will be considered later. Clearly the state of the world is sufficiently bad that little solace is gained by pointing out that the level of killing is not as bad as, say, during the western movement of Genghis Khan, when pyramids of skulls were left behind to mark despoiled capitals.

How might one carry out a war against misogyny? As a target misogyny is as widespread and vague as "terror" or just plain evil. Would a public that has accepted, to some degree, a worldwide war on terror be as ready to accept a war against misogyny? If images of Arabs can be used as icons for terrorism, what would be the icon for the classic misogynist? Altogether, the scale of current killing through war, genocide, and gynocide is enormous.

Is it fair to observe that there is no force good enough, neutral enough, rich enough, and large enough to stop the killing?

What the major powers are doing, however, is far from constructive. The members of the UN Security Council are among the most active merchants of weapons. To a significant degree, the economies of many nations rely on the manufacture and sale of more weapons, more technologically advanced weapons, more powerful weapons.

One might make at least two reasonable objections to the inventory in this chapter. Unlike the careful counts in various surveys, reported on a number of websites and in many publications, the count presented here is not carefully defined. It is in fact a decidedly un-careful and broad enumeration of killing. Because it is so broadly defined, there is little point in attempting to reach a final count of the dead, or to attempt to lay blame on specific continents or specific causes. However, one might attempt a rough estimate of the dead of the period from the beginning of the 20th century to the present. That total would include, at a minimum, all the dead women; World War II and the Holocaust; Mao's Great Leap Forward; Stalin's purges and forced migrations; the World War of Africa; all those killed in the recent wars in Iran, Iraq, Afghanistan, and Pakistan; the Vietnam War; the Korean War; the various conflicts among Vietnam, China, India, and Pakistan; and a congeries of post-colonial, ethnic, and colonial wars, as well as suppressions of liberation movements. An honest guess would be at least half a billion, or the equivalent of a quarter of the world's population in the early years of the twentieth century. This total is larger than some other estimates because it includes the war against women. Necrometrics.com compiles many estimates, including one that totals to 258 million for the twentieth entury. Pietro Scaruffi's website calculates 160 million for the twentieth century. Neither of these estimates factors in the backdrop, the war against women.

Second, the methodology here, or lack of methodology, is such that the count may as well include all those people killed in murders of one kind or another, whether motivated by love or family conflict or poverty or ethnicity or any other reason. The numbers game, as it is played by the statisticians, depends on narrowing rather than broadening the field of inquiry. Here the game of counting the dead has been played another way. The count is more inclusive. However one chooses to count the totals, it is abundantly clear that the current level of deaths in wars, civil wars and genocide is staggering and that the addition of more weapons to this ongoing holocaust is not likely to improve the situation. These wars are unwinnable by means of more violence.

To return to Joseph Popper's claim, any single life is worth more than all the art and science of human civilization. Any single life embodies a conscious understanding of the universe that is unique. Any one of these millions of deaths should be sufficient reason to limit the proliferation of weapons and the targeting of civilians.

Perhaps the North Sentinelese islanders were wise to keep to themselves.

4

Dragon's Teeth

"Dragon's Teeth" is a popular video game, or at least it was at the time this book was first drafted. Violent video games sell well around the world; their shelf life is limited. Like weapons, they are quickly replaced by new and better models. Military video games allow us to pretend that we are equipped with fearsome automatic weapons and the ability to kill people in large numbers with impunity, and even with safety, because we can always hit the reset button and give ourselves another life. Are there any video games in which a player is permanently killed and where the game ends with an officer arriving at the player's home to deliver the news to a sobbing family? Long distance drone fighting is like video games.

Each year there are contests where people pay to sit in theaters and play video games against each other. Perhaps these events are more exciting than going to see violent movies repeatedly, because each time the master players engage in battle, the story lines and the victors will change—a bit. (The US military provides violent video games to high schools as part of its recruiting effort, according to one of my students who worked for the army.) The original myth of dragon's teeth relates how the teeth of a slain dragon are sown on the ground, where they grow into fully armed warriors. To sow dragon's teeth is to raise up warriors and to foment violent conflict. In this chapter that myth is a lens for examining the way that weapons are sown about the earth where they can be picked up by anyone at all and used to exact staggering damage. Lately, the American press has featured an increasing number of stories about children picking up weapons: a nine-year old girl in Arizona who accidentally killed an instructor at a recreational gun range because she was unable to control the recoil of the Uzi submachine gun she had been handed, a two year old who took a gun from her mother's purse in a Walmart store and accidentally shot her mother to death.

No doubt there will be more long debates in the media and the academic press about the effects of virtual violence and the effects of the fascination with owning and playing with real weapons. Are there differences between playing with toy guns, as did children of the baby boom years, and spending time with a video monitor shooting images of people and blowing them to bits? Are these easy ways to let off tension or are these games training in aggression? Does it matter or not that the amount of certain kinds of violence increased in South Africa after television was finally introduced? Does it matter that when one sits in a hotel in Abu Dhabi the television stations are full of Pakistani music shows, American technology programs such as "Mythbusters," and recitations of the Qur'an rather than re-runs of American and European cops-and-robbers series replete with graphic violence? Do we become desensitized to violence? Is there a relationship between the widespread recreational use of video games and the tendency of television shows and movies to offer increasingly lurid violence to grab audiences' attention? Why do these questions even arise when of course there are many other activities on which people might spend their time and their manual dexterity? For example, learning to play the piano or the guitar demands the same kind of quick motor skills and responsiveness to inputs from sheet music and other performers.

A few years ago this author took a business trip to Abu Dhabi to work with the founders of a new educational institution. One night at about 2 a.m. I left my hotel when the temperature had dropped to the 80s. I walked around my immediate neighborhood. The humidity was still oppressive. I recalled how when I left the air-conditioned airport my glasses fogged over as soon as I stepped out into the moist air. In the hours after midnight the streets were full of people shopping, going to restaurants, standing in groups chatting. I speak almost no Arabic, so I had no idea what they were discussing, though their movements, tones of voices, and gestures as they conversed reminded me of the passeggiata in Italy: people in the neighborhood walking out into the street at dusk to share family news and to discuss whatever most impacts their lives. The crowds in Abu Dhabi were calm; in the heat even the salespeople showed little interest in pushing their wares. I walked to a small mini-mall and wandered through the shops. One sold video games and other toys. A boy about eight years old stood with his father looking through a display case window at a recently released video game. They both wore white dishidashas and head coverings. While they might have been engaged in serious moral discussion about the game for all I knew, from the little boy's enthusiasm I guessed that he wanted his father to buy him this latest battle game and that he understood computers well. I looked briefly over their shoulders as I walked by. The cover on the game showed American troops massacring Arabs, people who looked just like the little boy and his father, people who were dressed exactly like the little boy and his father in their white robes. The Americans were equipped with jet aircraft, tanks, rockets, automatic weapons, revolvers, flame-throwers, hand grenades, and other gear. The Arabs were aflame or covered in blood.

What would Americans think, I wondered, if Arab nations controlled the production of video games and marketed entertainments in which Arab or Islamist terrorists killed American soldiers? Wouldn't there be a roar of outrage from politicians on all sides about the inhumanity and insensitivity of teaching children to hate and kill people who look like us? Can anyone imagine a game in which Nazis won points for capturing Jews, for example, or in which KKK members got points for lynching African-Americans? There is no example too outrageous for this comparison. As the dominant culture, the West in general and America in particular think nothing apparently, of creating games for children that racially profile people in other civilizations, teach hatred of those people, and reward players who are children for killing and torturing those people. The West sows dragon's teeth; so does the East. Whatever we may profess about our care for others, our interest in the Islamic world, the fact is that the products we sell to children and to young adults teach them clearly that we view them with distrust, hatred, and a desire to erase their world.

Yes, it is a hideous over-reaction by Muslim fundamentalists when they kill a dozen people at a French satirical magazine, bomb nightclubs, or run over a crowd of people along the Promenade des Anglais in Nice. It would be more humbling to people in the West if the press around the world were to show pictures of the 500,000 noncombatants who have probably died as a result of the destruction of the civic infrastructure of Iraq, or if television showed pictures of Arab children playing at killing people who looked like them and their parents, games they bought at the local strip mall. Teaching others to hate themselves spares others the effort: as Richard Wright's *Black Boy* demonstrates repeatedly, self-policing is the most effective form of terrorism. In one scene of that book, Wright explains how a black elder finally took him aside to explain that the newspaper he had been conned into selling door to door in his neighborhood was a racist screed. Selling violent video games that target Arabs is little different from the more familiar forms of racism in American history.

In passing, it is worth noting that Americans sow dragon's teeth in their own nation, where weapons are easily and broadly available. That is what the Brady network tries to stop. At my own small American university, a psychotic young man from a nearby town, a man who had been psychiatrically hospitalized on several occasions, was allowed access to a hoard of weapons. He used a shotgun to kill a student on campus and to wound several others. He had hoped to kill many more, which he would have done if not for the courage of an engineering student, serving as a building monitor, who doused the killer's face with pepper spray and with the help of others tackled the killer and held him down until police arrived.

The 2007 Small Arms Survey published by the Graduate Institute of International and Development Studies in Geneva indicates that there are ninety-seven small arms for every 100 Americans, though of course those weapons are not evenly distributed. Some people own many; others own none. A more recent version of the same survey found eighty-eight small arms for every 100 Americans. The nation with the next most small arms per person is Serbia, site of a recent civil war and mass genocide, with about fifty-eight weapons per 100 citizens. Worldwide, according to the same organization's 2012 survey, there are about 875 million small arms in circulation, of which about 650 million are in private hands. That's about one weapon for every eight people worldwide, compared to nearly one for each person in the US. The 2015 Survey provides similar data. On average for the entire world, there are about ten guns for every one hundred people, or 1 weapon for every ten. In the United Kingdom, which has strict gun registration, there are 6.6 small arms per 100 persons. Anyone can look at a variety of sites on the Internet, for and against the ownership of weapons, and see that there is at least consensus on this point: that the United States is the developed nation with the highest rate of murder by guns. There are of course less developed nations with higher rates of killing, such as South Africa, Honduras, and about ten other sad nations. It is also true that private gun ownership statistics do not directly correlate either to war or to civil war. The Sudan, Afghanistan and the Democratic Republic of the Congo have fewer guns per person than Britain. Yet these nations are home to persistent wars and civil wars. Because low gun-ownership statistics do not guarantee an absence of gun violence, gun ownership advocates argue that more guns would be better than fewer guns, so that in September 2016, for example, students over the age of twenty-one who are licensed to own concealed weapons were able to bring their guns to class at universities throughout Texas. The thesis of this chapter is that where so many weapons are available worldwide, and where they can easily cross borders and be used to carry out wars and civil wars, the overall abundance of weapons contributes to the staggering number of wars and deaths that the world's population endures each year.

The simpler and somewhat less violent civilizations of the Karomojong of Uganda and the isolated North Sentinelese islanders have been mentioned earlier. Even Jared Diamond, the popular historian who attributes the movement of civilization to guns, germs, and steel, admits that alternatives to violent civilizations are possible, that not all civilizations have been violent, and that a civilization can become quite sophisticated without weapons. The people of Caral, on the coast of Peru, apparently lived for one thousand years in relative peace without any weapons at all. Their large structures were sometimes built by stacking net bags that contained small stones, rather than by cutting and stacking large stones. This method, in other words, was more attuned to individual or small group efforts rather than to massive, organized industries for cutting and moving large cut stones. No weapons have been found in the remains of the cities of Caral, only the long bones of deer that were pierced to make flutes; evidence of a diet of fish, fruits and vegetables; and the remains of plants reputed to be hallucinogenic and aphrodisiac. Caral was eventually assimilated into the Inca empire, though the native peoples who live in the area today still follow practices of the earlier culture.

Moreover, Caral may not have been that rare a phenomenon. Thomas Merton's study of the research on the Zapotec and Olmec cultures of Mexico and Central America suggest that while these peoples knew about war and had weapons, they did not go to war among themselves for a period that may have lasted as long as 2000 years: "the extraordinary thing about the Zapotec civilization of the Oaxaca Valley is that, like the Classic urban civilization of the Mayas and the so called 'Olmec' or Tenocelome culture, it maintained itself without war and without military power for many centuries. We can say that Monte Alban, in its pre-urban as well as its urban development, represents a peaceful and prosperous culture extending over two millennia without a full scale war and without any need for fortifications or a defense establishment" (67). Merton writes this in a book inspired by reflecting on the story of Ishi and the slaughter of his tribe by Americans coming into northern California.

How can one avoid the dangers of guns, germs, and steel? Is it possible not only that many civilizations thrived without metal weapons but also that the world as a whole would be more successful, more sustainable, more humane, if the quantities of weapons on hand were reduced? The United Nations believes so, and the UN plan for achieving this end will be examined later. And what if more people like the North Sentinelese, as violent as they are to protect their autonomy, were allowed to live according to their own lights? Steven Pinker's assessment of declining violence calls these people the Andamanese and emphasizes their warlike nature. We have no idea how they treat each other. All we know is that they seek to keep others away so that they may live in their own kind of peace.

Now dragon's teeth are strewn everywhere to help people defend themselves against real or imaginary threats. Making and selling weapons is not only big business, it is a major source of foreign exchange for many leading nations. Various agencies publish competing tallies of weapons sales. One might quote such lists for hundreds of pages. The brief enumeration presented here is designed to make two simple points: huge numbers of weapons of all kinds are manufactured and sold each year, and the nations that make the weapons derive enormous profits from this industry. Readers can surf the web and find numerous sites that will confirm and augment the data presented here. Of course the nations that profit from arms manufacture routinely speak of their commitments to peace and to their deep concern about the proliferation of nuclear weapons.

SmallArmsSurvey.org published its last regular report in 2015. Small arms as a category can include anything up through battlefield howitzers and some armored vehicles. Large arms include jet fighters, helicopters, and other complex systems such as warships and missiles. The authorized—that is legal—trade in small arms as of 2012 was $8.5 billion per year, a figure that had doubled in the period 2001–2011. About half of that amount was ammunition. The Stockholm International Peace Research Institute (SIPRI) analysis of arms transfers in 2011 tallied $43 billion in trade that year. That agency's "Top List" of nations *transferring* arms included Russia ($8.2 billion), the United States ($6.2 billion), China ($1.8 billion), Italy ($800 million), Israel ($800 million), Spain ($600 million), the Ukraine ($600 million), Sweden ($500 million) and Belarus ($340 million). These figures have been rounded to the nearest billion or million.

The *New York Times*, reporting on a paper produced by the Congressional Research Service, however, indicates that the United States sold $66.3 billion in weapons and weapons contracts in 2011. That amount was three quarters of the total arms sales in the world for the year. Transfers evidently differ from contracts and sales, because weapons can be given away or traded as well as sold, and the contracts that were signed that year may have involved payments over many years. In fact, the United States donates large numbers of weapons each year that are paid for by US taxpayers. Those who are interested can pursue these details. In 2016, *Time*, citing the same annual federal report, noted that the US was still the top arms merchant in the world, claiming 50% of the market in 2014. In 2014, the US sold $36.2 billion in weapons, followed by Russia with $10.2 billion, Sweden with $5.5 billion, France with $4.4 billion and China with $2.2 billion. The *New York Times* also reported that in 2014 Saudi Arabia purchased a total of $80 billion of weapons, including large systems such as helicopters and fighter jets. The *Manchester Guardian* reported that weapons sales to the Gulf States had risen 70% in the five years leading to 2015. A later chapter of this book considers the effect of such budgetary commitments when these nations face huge drops in the price of oil that force the nations to cut back on employment and social services because of arms purchases.

GlobalIssues.org reports that the five permanent members of the United Nations Security Council are responsible for the majority of weapons sales, a point that argues against using that organization for peacekeeping. If the Security Council consists of weapons merchants, what do they gain from peace? This may seem a naïve question. However, the vast amounts spent on weapons indicate that the question is worth posing and needs to be answered. GlobalIssues' tally of arms sales for the period 2004–1011 lists the percentage of arms sales that can be attributed to each nation: US, 44%; Russia, 17%; France, 8%; United Kingdom, 5%; Germany 4%; Italy, 3%, Other European nations, 10%; Other nations, 10%. Chief buyers were Saudi Arabia, 21%, India, 13%; and the United Arab Emirates, 6%.

The importance of weapons sales to the American economy can be estimated by considering that in the first quarter of 2014, according to the Bureau of Economic Analysis of the US Department of Commerce, the United States was running a $111.2 billion trade deficit. Without those considerable arms sales, the economic situation of the US would be much more compromised. For the whole of 2014, the trade deficit was $342.6 billion, offset by $36.2 billion in weapons sales. For 2015, the total trade deficit was $531.5 billion, offset partially by $46.6 billion in weapons sales. The Geneva Declaration on Armed Violence and Development published a report covering the years 2000–2010. Titled "Global Burden of Armed Violence, 2015," it noted that the estimated economic losses due to armed violence came to $2 trillion, with a death rate of 7.4 deaths per 100,000, or 508,000 dead by armed violence per year. This works out to about $200 billion in economic losses each year. The numbers cited above are difficult to compare, because sales income can come in over many years, and the criteria for every aspect of these numbers vary from one report to another. If the US sold about half the weapons in 2014, total weapons sales for the year might have been in the range of $75 billion, so that if one takes into account the economic cost of damage by weapons, then every dollar spent on weapons created another $2.67 in fresh damage somewhere on the planet.

What nations sell, however, is only part of the story. According to William Hartung, in a report written for the conservative Cato Institute, the United States gives away a huge quantity of weapons and helps to finance the weapons that it sells. Hartung's 1999 analysis indicated that half of US weapons sales were financed by US taxes. Records from 1996 showed that out of $12 billion in sales that year, $7.9 billion of weapons sales were financed by the US government. Beneficiaries of these programs included Turkey, Colombia, Zaire, Egypt, Israel, Albania, Cambodia, Bulgaria, the Czech Republic, Estonia, Greece, Georgia, Hungary, Jordan, Kazakhstan, Kyrgyzstan, Latvia, Lithuania, Macedonia, Moldova, Poland, Romania, Russia, Slovakia, Slovenia, Turkmenistan, Ukraine and Uzbekistan. In addition, during fiscal year 1997, the Pentagon "gave away military equipment with an original acquisition value of $973 million" (Hartung, 8).

Perhaps included in national weapons budgets are the funds spent on the development of weapons that are abandoned or whose production is canceled. Or perhaps some of these expenditures are accounted for under other budgets. The spider's web of connections is complex. Money spent on space research and related weapons research has often been rationalized in terms of the benefits to civilian life, such as advancements in medical care due to the development of micro-technologies. Without examining that rationalization in detail, one can make a simple, blunt, and satirical observation. Suppose that a nation were to invest billions of dollars in the development of a superior mayonnaise. The argument might run that even though the mayonnaise was not an improvement on previous mayonnaise, and even though none of the experimental mayonnaises reached production, chemists learned a great deal of value about oil molecules that could be applied to the treatment of atherosclerosis and the improvement of internal combustion engines. Perhaps, in such a weird scenario, that money would have been better spent directly on health care and energy efficiency. So too, one has a right to be somewhat skeptical of the indirect value of space research and weapons research.

The facts are also that a great deal of money is spent developing weapons that never reach production because they are superseded or fail to meet their objectives. Jeremy Bauder's essay in Business Insider in January 2016 listed fifteen of the "most expensive projects abandoned by the US military," which totaled $51.2 billion in development without "any field systems to show for it." Stephen Rodriguez, in a similar essay for the website War on the Rocks, lists ten systems developed in the "Revolution in Military Affairs" era that were dropped, totaling $53 billion in expenditures. Forbes magazine in 2011 published an essay on "How to Waste $100 Billion" on useless weapons systems. Debate continues in Congress about the utility of the new F-35 fighter, as well as its ability to meet its design criteria, and journalists and experts have published lists of other current projects that are likely to be canceled because of cost, design flaws, or redundancy. Most recently, in late July 2016, there are reports that the new $13 billion US aircraft carrier, the Gerald Ford, first of several Ford-class aircraft carriers, was unable to fulfill its mission because its electronic systems do not function adequately. If the one trillion dollars and counting that have been spent by the United States in Iraq in recent years were divided evenly among the fifty American states, each state would have had about $20 billion to spend, which is enough to carry out major improvements to infrastructure, health care, or education. Rather than being wasted, or stolen, or blown up, that money could have built facilities that would last generations, the way that the projects of the Depression years still grace American communities with high school stadiums, dams, hydroelectric generators, highways, parks, public hospitals, community clinics, schools, public art, and museums. There is material for a lifetime of grieving in contemplating what has been lost through this extravagant waste of national resources on weapons and warfare that has been used to harm others and to damage other nations in ways that will require generations to repair. All without any clear evidence of progress toward whatever dimly limned goals have been articulated, and all while the Earth's citizens have denied ourselves desperately needed national improvements in infrastructure, health care, education, and other areas of high priority. What is true for the United States is also true for other nations that have spent such fortunes on the development of weapons.

Economic cost is another way to measure the cost of war. The UNDP Post Conflict Economic Recovery Crisis Prevention and Recovery Report for 2008 estimates that at any time thirty-five nations are in post-conflict recovery. Estimates of economic recovery times for nations to recover economically from a civil wars differ widely. The average for some satisfactory level of recovery may be a mere ten years. The recovery time for human relations, however, cannot be calculated, because we have too many examples of nations where ethnic conflicts have continued for as long as we have history. Paul Collier's Development and Conflict paper, published by his Oxford University website, estimates that a typical civil war lasts ten years and costs $50 billion, with about two new civil wars starting every year.

No doubt some of the weapons that are sold each year become useless or broken, yet many remain, along with both aging and new stocks of ammunition, to be wielded by whomever manages to secure them. They can be bought for bitcoins, a useful anonymous currency, on websites maintained by weapons dealers around the world, although a survey of stories about this market suggests that sales have tailed off because of the difficulty of delivering weapons through the mail. Other commodities are more easily delivered.

The United States armed Iraq against Iran and then fought Iraq. The United States armed Iraq again; the Iraqi army has lost large amounts of those munitions to soldiers for the new Caliphate or ISIS or ISIL; the US is now fighting the Caliphate. The United States armed Afghan fighters against the Soviet Union and has been fighting Afghan groups for over thirteen years. A US Inspector General's report issued in 2014 indicates that about 43% of the weapons provided to Afghanistan ended up in the hands of persons later considered to be enemies. Another way to measure that same loss is that it amounts to over $400 million in arms, and somewhere (depending on the estimate one consults) between 112,000 excess weapons or 200,000 lost weapons. It is feared, moreover, that many of the weapons provided to anti-Assad forces in the Syrian civil war are going to the Caliphate (or ISIS, ISIL, or Daech), and that much of the military aid given to Pakistan is also diverted to forces aligned against American interests. Given this sorry record, is it necessary to leaf back through the pages of history into the late twentieth century and before to examine how often these large supplies of weapons have been used against those who manufactured and sold them? What nations build and sell is often used against them.

In the late summer of 2014, another specter arose. When Egypt and the United Arab Emirates began to use their formidable advanced weapons, purchased from the US and other Western and Eastern powers, to attack Islamists in Libya, without notifying the United States of their plans—without, in other words, showing deference to the single superpower—there arose the possibility that those vast stocks of aircraft, missiles, and other equipment manufactured and sold by the United States and others may begin to be used freely across international borders by new players and governments who wish to engage in their own "right to respond" when and wherever they choose. Suddenly, in the American press at least, the idea of other people exercising a universal right to attack evil anywhere did not seem as reasonable as it did when it was understood that Americans were the only people who could arrogate that right to themselves. What did we expect nations like the United Arab Emirates to do with all those jets and advanced weapons they were buying? Is there an agency that has a long-term perspective on the consequences of what has been set in place in terms of conventional weapons, not to mention nuclear weapons and other long-lasting threats such as land mines? While the international campaign against land mines is important, those mines are merely a metaphor for the trillions of dollars of other kinds of weapons that are silent and waiting to be used all over the world, from inexpensive hand guns to fighter-bombers.

When one considers the disconnect between nations that buy weapons and nations that are currently using weapons, a terrible question arises. The next chapter of this book will examine some aspects of the recent history of the Sultanate of Oman, a progressive Arab nation that occupies a strategic place in the world, though it is not a nation that receives much news coverage. When a nation such as Oman spends 11.8% of its national budget on weapons and yet is not apparently engaged in direct combat, then what is the purpose of the expenditure? Certainly in the case of Oman, the fact that it overlooks the Strait of Hormuz between Arabia and Iran is significant. Certainly Oman's border with Yemen is important, as is its place along the southeastern coast of Arabia, where across the Red Sea it faces nations such as Somalia, where piracy on the seas has become a serious problem. Is it fair to suggest, however, that arms purchases by Arab states constitute a kind of insurance policy that keeps the United States engaged in their defense?

The United States has sent huge numbers of its own troops to fight in wars that are part of an ongoing competition between Sunni and Shiite Islam. That conflict is more the personal business of the various Arab states and Persian Iran than the direct business of the United States. Are nations induced to buy weapons they may not use in order to keep revenue flowing to the American military-industrial complex? Are these nations in effect buying American mercenary soldiers to fight their wars, or to fight wars that America thinks those nations should be fighting?

However, the toll of weapons is greater, because many nations buy guns that divert money from desperately needed national needs. World Data Bank listed the nations in 2014 that had spent the largest proportion of their GDPs on weapons;

Nation	%
Sultanate of Oman	11.8%
Saudi Arabia	10.8%
Libya	8%
United Arab Emirates	5.7%
Algeria	5.5%
Israel	5.2%
Democratic Republic of the Congo	5%
Iraq	4.3%
United States	3.5%

Thomas Piketty estimates that a typical nation spends 2% to 3% of its national budget on its military, a figure that includes not merely weapons purchases but also all the other expenses of recruiting, training, and maintaining military forces, equipment, bases, and their associated expenses (628). If one examines the weapons budgets of nations side by side with their educational and health care budgets, the real cost of weapons begins to become clearer. What is spent on weapons cannot be spent on national infrastructure, education, economic development, health, transportation, and other priorities. The toll on one national economy is the subject of the next chapter.

It is evident that weapons sold across the world will continue to exist and that there is no way to predict who will control them in the future. The very presence of these weapons has the power to transform cultures from ones in which there are limited levels of violence into ones where violence

Dragon's Teeth

is widely fatal and where attitudes about what is acceptable change quickly when people obtain the technologies of death that allow them to kill large numbers of people with ease. What our capacity to adjust to violence says about the human race as a species is not at issue. The bare fact is that these adjustments take place and that the result is that we are prepared to watch films with violence that would have shocked our parents, play games that would shock earlier generations, and carry out massacres that would appall earlier generations with their speed, size and callousness. Yes, Ghengis Khan and other invaders killed in vast numbers. They stacked skulls, as did the more recent killers in Cambodia. We have now made that kind of slaughter easy and mechanical. We have made the means for such killing available across the planet.

Land mines have received much attention in recent years. Land mines can retain their explosive power for decades, just like bombs from World War II that are still unearthed in Germany, France, England and elsewhere. Land mines are only a fraction of the problem of dragon's teeth. The full problem includes the whole range of weapons in existence, from small arms to nuclear weapons.

The United Nations has a plan to address the problem of weapons. In its January 2009 UN Chronicle, Small Arms: No Single Solution, the UN wisely lays out steps that might be taken. These include reducing the stockpile of weapons worldwide, destroying weapons, and reducing the supply. This a good plan. The question raised by this book is whether we have designed a world whose economy depends on the sale of weapons.

In the United States, that question is answered in part by examining the data on lobbying carried out by weapons manufacturers. The National Rifle Association in 2015 spent $3.6 million lobbying (Open Secrets). The arms industry spent $25 million on lobbying during the 2013–2014 election cycle (Arms Industry Ramps Up). During 2015, according to Open Secrets, the Defense-Aerospace industry spent over $74 million for lobbying, and *Time* magazine reported that this spending was up 25% from 2011 to 2015. Statista.com confirms the number reported by Open Secrets: $74 million in 2015. Recently, much of this lobbying has focused on ending caps on military spending. In the case of the controversial F35 fighter jet, the reason for the large number of lobbyists can be found in the number of jobs created by the fighter program. According to a report by Tess VandenDolder in Streetwise, the F 35 project involves 133,000 jobs in 45 American states and could grow to providing 260,000 jobs. It is frankly hard to credit these large numbers. If indeed they are true, they indicate the degree to which the American economy is tied to the weapons industry. The US builds more weapons than any other nation. The lobbyists are getting what they pay for, and it appears that the decision-making processes and priorities of the American government are skewed.

An additional aspect of lobbying is the "revolving door," the number of public officials and government staffers who leave to take jobs in various industries. According to OpenSecrets.com, in 2014 a mere 3.8% of these individuals revolved into the defense industry; most went into other sectors, including pharmaceuticals. Officials who accept paid positions in companies must have the assignment reviewed by a federal ethics agency, Between January 2012 and May 2013, there were 379 such ethics reviews for federal employees who had been offered employment in the defense industry (Politico, Project on Government Oversight). Officials who work as outside consultants, however, are not required to undergo an ethics review.

The evidence supports the claims that the world's major nations are responsible for manufacturing and selling weapons to the remainder of the world, that these weapons are often used against the interests of those who make them, and that the economies of major nations are closely tied to weapons manufacture. The proliferation of weapons is an inducement to continued warfare.

5

Economic Imbalance and the Weapons Trade

Money spent on weapons is money not spent on other national priorities. These other priorities include health care and the kinds of education that can lift nations out of resource-dependent economies into more advanced economies. In some nations, goals for mathematics education are set very low. Governments hope that the poor can calculate change and manage simple balance sheets in order to run elementary businesses, such as roadside shops. Most of the world's nations do not participate in the PISA (Program for International Student Assessment) tests that measure the mathematical competence of citizens.

The 2012 PISA scores indicate that, with the exception of the Ukraine, all of the major weapons suppliers participate in the international educational race. Those nations are the US, Russia, France, the UK, Israel, Italy, Sweden and China. Not one of the poorer nations that buy large numbers of weapons participated in PISA that year: Oman, Algeria, Congo, Iraq, Morocco, South Sudan. Of the rich nations that bought large quantities of weapons, Saudi Arabia, Bahrain and the UAE, only the UAE participated in PISA. Without adequate mathematical education, people cannot learn the skills necessary to participate in any of the STEM disciplines: science, technology, engineering, and mathematics. Without citizens who are adept in STEM fields, nations cannot participate in the growing technological economy. It is doubtful that any nation deliberately carries out war by trying to impede educational progress elsewhere in the world, though when assistance is given in the form of weapons rather than in the form of help to build educational institutions, the effect is the same. Developing nations are kept down.

While working on a book on doctoral education across the globe, this author was told by a specialist from one large nation that will not be named that if 90% of the universities in his country were closed, it would not make any difference at all, because the standard of education was so low that 98% of the professors of technical subjects in his country could not pass the entrance exams given by international technical corporations to screen employment candidates. Comments of this kind may be exaggerations, but they point to a major emerging problem with the ability of all nations to participate in the technological economy. Thomas Piketty argues that "unequal access to higher education...is one of the most important problems that social states everywhere must face in the twenty-first century" (485).

Ratings of universities are notoriously complex and controversial. What is less controversial is the geographic distribution of universities that are considered, by almost all measures, to be leading centers of research and development. The Shanghai Jiao Tong ranking of world universities is based on such measures as the number of Nobel Prize winners, winners of other major prizes, and above all the number of patents and citations of research papers. In other words, the Shanghai rating focuses on intellectual and technological productivity. The fact that Shanghai performs this complex rating process indicates the seriousness with which the Chinese government takes the task of equaling or topping the productivity and quality of major universities elsewhere. The top twenty universities on that annual list tend to be seventeen American research universities, the University of Tokyo, Oxford and Cambridge. If one looks for the rankings of universities in nations where there is significant conflict, almost none make the list of 500. Those that do include King Abdulaziz University, King Fahd University and King Saud University in Saudi Arabia; the Indian Institute of Science; Cairo University; Istanbul University; and Stellenbosch and Witwatersrand in South Africa. Of course those nations, Saudi Arabia, Turkey, Egypt, South Africa and India, are not currently facing invasions, though they are involved in conflicts or social upheavals, and in some cases are waging wars or involved in regional wars. Ratings by the Center for World University Rankings and Webometrics.info indicate similar results. There is little research and development taking place at universities in the global south, in the Arab world, in Central and Eastern Europe, and in most of Asia. Iran's best universities rank in the 900s on the Center for

Economic Imbalance and the Weapons Trade

World University Rankings list. Nations actually at war tend to close their universities, because they are often centers of perceived or real agitation.

The Sultanate of Oman offers an excellent case study because it is a nation that virtually fell off the map and because it is a conservative though progressive Islamic nation, part of the civilization that sees itself as an alternative to the limitations of the West. As the head of the national law school told this author, Islamic civilization has been asleep for seven hundred years, and now it is waking up. For a long time Oman was so obscure that a 1970's book about the Middle East failed to show Oman on the map and provided not a word about this currently important nation, whose coastline stretches roughly 1000 miles from Yemen in the south to the United Arab Emirates in the north. Inland, Oman borders the Rub al Khali, the Empty Quarter of Arabia that is primarily under the control of Saudi Arabia. Oman is also separated from Saudi Arabia by a mountain range that rises to over 10,000 feet. Oman has strategic importance because it borders the Red Sea, where there is active piracy, Yemen, where there have been ongoing civil wars, and most important the Strait of Hormuz, where a large proportion (40%) of the world's oil passes through a narrow channel with Iran on one side and Oman on the other. The Sultan of Oman's assistance and mediation were critical to the development of a treaty between Iran and the United States that has begun to bring an end to a generation of hostility. Oman does not have large oil reserves. They can be compared to the remaining oil reserves of the Scandinavian nations. Oman does have large natural gas fields. However the gas is spread over a huge territory and the wells bring up enormous quantities of brackish water that must be managed. Like the other Gulf States, Oman is working assiduously to develop a more diverse economy for the years that will follow the decline of oil revenue.

Historically, Oman is probably the source of the copper that provided Mesopotamia with the metal necessary to enter the Bronze Age. Oman is the also the home of the legends associated with Sinbad the Sailor. Although it was never a British colony or protectorate, Oman was under British influence after periods as a Portuguese colony during the Age of Discovery and then a monarchy that controlled territories in what are now Pakistan and Tanzania. For most of the twentieth century, Oman was ruled by a Sultan who lived in the resort town of Salalah, some 500 miles from his capital in Muscat. The Sultan personally signed all entry and exit visas, which meant in practice that the country was nearly inaccessible, and he kept his son, who was educated at Sandhurst, the British equivalent of West Point, under house arrest. The country had six miles of paved road, endemic malaria, unsafe drinking water, and one twenty-five bed hospital. The tall wooden gates of the capital city were locked each night, and in the absence of electric light, those who walked the streets were required to carry lanterns. People caught without lanterns were arrested and presumed to be thieves. The old Sultan was served by African slaves who were required to shave their heads so that their status was clear at all times. The British maintained an air base outside Salalah during World War II that was used to fly reconnaissance missions over the Indian Ocean, and British and American air force units occasionally used other sites in the country or on the island of Masirah, off the coast, in the Red Sea. The British army helped the Sultan through a rebellion in which the leader of the nation's Islamic majority sect, the Ibadi, sought to separate Oman's interior from the coastal capital and perhaps unify with Saudi Arabia. In the late 1960s, the Sultan was embroiled in a long war with Communist insurgents from Yemen. He received help from Britain and from the Shah of Iran. In many respects, Oman was primitive and out of touch with modernity.

In 1970, with British assistance, the current Sultan Qaboos sent his father into exile in England and assumed control. Sultan Qaboos understood that creating stability in his nation meant a huge, careful, and gradual investment in the economy, public services, and infrastructure. Omanis who lived through Qaboos' "Renaissance" are sometimes speechless when they reflect on how much has been accomplished in a mere forty-odd years. Qaboos might have survived if he had done nothing; he might have followed in the path of kleptocrats like Mobutu Sese Soko, funneling national resources to Swiss bank accounts. Instead, he functions as a technocrat and a micromanager. There is of course corruption and favoritism, as in any nation, and within the last few years, Oman has been forced to deal with fallout from some failed resort and housing projects. Complaints during the Arab Spring focused on employment, with heavy support for the Sultan himself, though international groups have expressed concern about the slow pace at which the Sultan has been willing to introduce more public freedoms and democratic processes. Omani intellectuals, for example, complain about living in a nation where a micro-manager makes so many routine decisions by himself rather than relying on a wider pool of citizens. Like other Gulf Nations, Oman struggles to replace foreign technical workers with locally educated citizens, which requires the development of a stronger K-PhD educational system, the imposition of national educational standards, and the achievement of educational outcomes that are comparable to those in the developed world.

Today this nation of four million people, up from about 650,000 in 1970, can boast an extensive system of paved roads, a freeway from the international airport into Muscat, safe water, electricity, free public education through high school, a royal decree that half of all students in the national university must be women, free college for those admitted to the 18,000 plus student national university, free national health care, and high rankings in various international studies of freedom and happiness. The economy grew from $256 million in 1970 to nearly $80 billion in 2012 (Globalriskinsights.com). The endemic diseases have been largely eradicated. Oman, however, is one of just three nations in the world that does not provide any paid maternity leave: the other two nations that provide no paid maternity leave are Papau New Guinea and the United States of America. (Depending on the source, there is some ambiguity about this claim. It may be that only Papua New Guinea and the United States merit this distinction.) As noted and as in other Gulf nations, there is an emphasis on training local citizens to take over jobs that have been held by foreign nationals. Through this educational and employment initiative as through other programs, the nation focuses on sustainability, on what industries will keep it running when its oil and gas reserves have been used. In many ways the nation is a model of what can be achieved with somewhat limited resources, clear priorities and highly focused leadership. The case of Oman may also indicate what can be achieved in smaller nations with ethnic homogeneity, because a tribal system is still in place and citizens are very much raised by villages of people to whom they are related. Finland and Iceland offer similar examples. In those nations the national educational systems and their funding are driven by national initiatives to develop specific kinds of industries and the technical expertise that will allow those nations to prosper in the face of technological competition from the United States and from other larger and technically advanced economies, and in the face of competitive labor costs in China, Vietnam and other developing areas of the world where labor is cheap.

The story of Oman, like the stories of contemporary Iceland and Finland, raises profound questions about the conditions necessary for nationwide planning and the execution of plans. Is there a size beyond which no nation should grow if it is to be governable? The downsides to Oman's success are also apparent. Projects start and stop as the national budget has funding available, priorities change, and goals are not always met. The Muscat Daily, an online paper, reported that in 2012, the math scores of Omani students were among the lowest in the world, with a rank of 73 out of 85 nations that participated in one international examination (Thomas). Low educational achievement makes it very difficult for the nation to replace foreign experts with locally trained specialists.

Unlike many European and South American nations that have been able to cut military budgets, Oman also has a very large defense budget. The table presented in the previous chapter tells a sobering story. In 2014, Oman spent a larger percentage of its national budget on weapons than any other nation on the planet. The total dollar amount was of course lower than the expenditure of Saudi Arabia, which spent the next highest percentage. Yet that percentage of the budget, in a nation where spending is limited and where decisions are made with an understanding of what cannot be bought and what projects must be postponed to fund other priorities, means that Oman had to cut back in other areas. It is not clear how much of that expenditure is truly necessary for national defense. The United States gave Oman $14 million in military aid in 2014. There is a fresh civil war in bordering Yemen as well as significant Islamist activity in Yemen. Oman maintains good relations with Iran. Oman, however, must deal with the threat posed by pirates in the Red Sea and the Indian Ocean. Did the nation truly need to upgrade its air force? Did it need to spend 11.8% of its national budget on new arms?

The weapons issue in Oman is one of military spending, not personal spending on small arms. Small Arms Survey reports that there is about one small arm in the country for every four residents. The World Crime and Safety Index for mid-year 2016 reports that Oman has a crime index of 25.85 (lower is better on a scale of 0 to 100), which can be compared to the United States, with a crime index of 48.68 and the United Kingdom, with a crime index of 42.37. The weapons problem in Oman is not public ownership of weapons but rather the nation's degree of preparedness for some future war.

Oman was managing reasonably well and avoiding debt until the recent fall in oil prices. When oil prices fell drastically, however, the nation was forced to begin a process of radical cutbacks. A daily reading of the official national online newspaper, *The Times of Oman*, reveals the ongoing costs. The price of Omani oil dropped 38%, which led to a national current account deficit (EulerHermes). Petroleum accounted in 2016 for 64% of the nation's export income and 50% of the GDP (Gulfbase.com). Not only were oil prices lower, oil sales also dropped, and oil exploration projects were halted. As a result, national infrastructure and development projects have been postponed. Workers' benefits have been cut. Jobs have been cut back, in spite of the fact that during Arab Spring there were protests in the streets calling for more and better employment.

Roughly half of the Omani population is ex-patriots: 1.6 million ex-patriot workers from many parts of the developed and developing world, including many people from Pakistan, India, and other areas of South Asia. Many of these workers were told that they would not be permitted to change jobs. They had to work for the employer who recruited them or leave the country. Obviously, whatever bargaining power those workers possessed was lost. Some workers whose contracts ended were "banned" from the country, which meant that they were not permitted to find other jobs in Oman and were forced to leave Oman for at least two years before being allowed to return. The nation announced a goal of reducing the percentage of ex-patriot workers in Oman from 39% of the labor force to 33% (GulfBusiness). On a rough estimate, this means deporting about 120,000 ex-patriot workers, when it may not be clear whether the remaining ex-patriot and Omani population is either willing or ready to take over the jobs once filled by those who depart. Removing people from the country is a way of managing deficits. As a policy it is a starkly realistic way of controlling costs. It is in some ways comparable to recent proposals to deport large numbers of undocumented aliens from the United States without considering the effect either on those people themselves or on the individual businesses and industries that will be left without skilled or unskilled labor that may be difficult to replace.

It is a credit to Oman that the government publicly announced these changes in priorities while at the same time explaining why policy changes were necessary. From a distance, it is difficult, however, to measure the short and long term effects of such radical changes in employment and benefits for Omani citizens and for ex-patriot workers. How are their pay and benefits changing? What other cuts in services have been made to accommodate budgetary deficits? In the face of these challenges, how much has Oman's enormous expenditure on weapons cost the nation's health and development? How do these changes affect the stability of Oman's economy and the attitudes of customers and of outside investors? Oman's Renaissance is one of the most remarkable transformations of a country in the twentieth century. The Sultanate grew from a primitive state to a modern power, to a large degree because of the leadership of a careful planner and manager, the Sultan himself. When the Sultan dies, he has no heir. He has left two letters offering guidance on who should succeed him. There is no guarantee that the next Sultan will be as forward thinking and as careful with national resources. As he enters old age, the shock to the oil market has put many of his plans on hold and has destabilized the employment market. Just as these economic threats emerged, Oman had decided to invest a huge amount of its national treasure in new weapons. Without more information, it is not possible to draw firm conclusions about the ways in which commitments to weapons purchases have contributed to the slump in the national economy. Still, it seems reasonable to assert that weapons purchases have very likely taken resources from projects that are fundamentally more important to the long-term security and economic development of Oman. Full employment, continued public services, progress toward diversifying the economy, oil and gas exploration and development, and better educational outcomes are arguably more significant contributions to national security than upgrades to an already large military establishment.

While the troubles facing Oman are important and demonstrate the dangers of high military spending, Saudi Arabia's current situation is similar and far more important from a global perspective, because of the size of Saudi Arabia's population, its position in the middle of conflict, and its enormous oil revenue. Saudi Arabia has released its Vision 2030 plan, which is designed to address the economic pressures faced by the kingdom due to decreased oil revenues, increasing population, relatively high unemployment, and a high need to develop a diversified economy. Paul Sullivan, a scholar who specializes in the region, prepared an assessment of the Vision 2030 plan for the National Council on US-Arab Relations. His analysis underscores the danger of military investment. Saudi Arabia spent 10.8% of its national budget on weapons in 2014, not as high a percentage as small Oman, but obviously a much larger amount of money.

Sullivan begins his analysis by stating that oil revenue represents 35–45% of the Saudi national budget and between 85% and 90% of the nation's export revenue. Demand for oil is expected to be flat, with a decline in the Chinese economy and very heavy pressure elsewhere to move away from carbon-based fuels. It takes a price of $10 a barrel for the Saudi oil industry to break even on production costs. A price of $100 per barrel is required by the nation's typical annual budget. Therefore the gap between a $60–$80 price per barrel and the need for a price of $100 per barrel presents Saudi Arabia with a very significant economic challenge. (As of August 2016, that international price dropped below $40 per barrel.) The Kingdom plans to develop mining in addition to solar- and wind-power capacity. Saudi Arabia has dedicated between 23% and 25% of its national budget to education, though its top universities have yet to enter the top 100, as measured by the Shanghai Jai Tong University ranking of university research productivity. Like other Arab nations, Saudi Arabia also faces difficulties inducing nationals to enter the competitive private sector and to eschew the benefits of government jobs. About half of Saudi university students drop out, which can be compared to an American university drop out rate of about 42%, according to the Calder Center. The American drop out rate is considered an emergency by some. The severe limitations placed on women who wish to work also constitute a problem for Saudi Arabia, according to Sullivan. The Vision 2030 plan calls for 30% of women to work. It also calls for development of religious and non-religious tourism, much larger private-sector involvement in economic development, and foreign investment. However, the research infrastructure and fully qualified workers are not yet present to the degree necessary. Moreover, cultural and religious barriers militate against increases in female employment and tourism. Fundamentalist Wahhabi Islam still dominates the culture and limits the participation of women in public life.

Saudi Arabia faces major challenges. Against this background, the 10.8% of the national budget spent on weapons becomes a drag on development opportunities. Saudi Arabia in 2016 was still at war in Yemen. And Saudi Arabia imports almost all of its military equipment and weapons, so that turning to local production is not an easy option.

The cases of Oman and Saudi Arabia underscore a simple global truth: money spent on weapons is money that is not spent on other national priorities. These choices can result in destabilizing nations and increasing the risk of civil discord.

6

Just War?

The Failure of International Treaties

The world has attempted to control the use of weapons in war for nearly two millennia. My previous book, *Blessed are the Pacifists: The Beatitudes and Just War Theory*, took issue with the limitations of "just war theory" and also with the limitations of the late Glen Stassen's "just peacemaking theory." Just war theory begins with St. Augustine and with the problems faced by Christianity as an institution when it became the official religion of the Roman Empire. Suddenly rather than being a pacifistic protest movement, Christianity was a state institution, and there could be Christian soldiers and judges, so it was necessary to develop a body of thought about the limits that Christians needed to observe when they assumed these tasks and duties, if they chose to do so. Just war theory encompasses a set of principles that have grown and changed over time. Before a war, there must be a just cause, such as self-defense, and the situation must have reached a state where there is no other choice other than accepting defeat. War is a last resort. There should also be a clear and limited objective for any war. Wars should not develop into programs of nation building, or conquest, or cultural transformation. In the case of the American invasion of Afghanistan, for example, the initial objective of finding the leaders of the attack on New York morphed into an effort to guarantee some kind of liberal democracy and to guarantee the free education of women, a project that involves changing foundational elements of Afghan culture. Whether those goals should be pursued for some high ethical reason is not the issue here; the issue is whether going to war and using the military as a change agent is appropriate.

Some argue that those who go to war must have a specific status, such as being a recognized nation. On this basis, the American Revolution might be considered unjust, because the revolutionaries were not a well-established political entity. However, the American government decided during its war in Afghanistan that some combatants did not merit any of the benefits of various treaties and conventions, because those combatants were not representatives of an official government. For that reason, those individuals were imprisoned in Guantanamo Bay. Within war itself, there should be provisions to protect noncombatants, to limit damage to what is proportional to the objective, and to use weapons that are "just" in the sense of doing no more damage than is necessary to achieve the objective. After the war is over, there should be a system for establishing justice and dealing with excesses. There should also be efforts to re-build what has been damaged or destroyed. Glen Stassen's just peacemaking theory adds to these principles a set of guidelines for when outsiders, whether nations or individuals, should seek to support liberation movements and movements for justice. Without examining those principles in detail, they tend to be based on Western, democratic values and to be framed in terms of ways that people in the developed world, primarily the Western world, can intervene in the affairs of developing nations and introduce Western values. Many Muslims, including progressive Muslims, believe in the superiority of their cultural and moral systems. Those who advocate for the imposition of some form of Western values should be required both to articulate those values and to consider the virtue of imposing them on a competing civilization. Many Americans are currently concerned about what they perceive to be efforts to impose Sharia law in America, and yet those same people seem not to comprehend the reaction of those on whom American groups wish to impose their values. Just Peacemaking theory, in other words, requires a sustained argument for the superiority of whatever form of Western civilization and economy that Westerners wish to impose. That argument may be hard to sustain in the face of the visions of other cultures and also because of the clear imperfections of Western cultures.

More recently, just war theory and just peacemaking theory have been joined by what some have called the right to respond doctrine, which seems to overrule the earlier theories, and by the responsibility to protect theory, which is a project to inculcate a series of principles that can be used by nations to respond to instances where there is strong evidence that genocide or civil war are about to break out and large numbers of people are in danger. Right to respond is a defense of military incursions articulated by some members of the American military, with the understanding that it confers a direct right to invade where there is danger to civilians. It is an interpretation of the Bush Doctrine articulated by President George W. Bush in September, 2002. That doctrine (how curious that a term with strong religious connotations is adopted for these pronouncements) claims the right to engage in preventive war, to take unilateral action, and to spread democracy and freedom.

Responsibility to protect is specifically targeted against crimes of mass atrocity, including genocide, war crimes, ethnic cleansing, and crimes against humanity. All of these four kinds of crimes, which are often overlapping, are defined in terms of how widespread are the effects.

While the development of this theory, its support by the United Nations, and the creation of a UN Office of the Special Adviser on the Prevention of Genocide are all positive steps for the world community, this development is not without limitations. Among them are the criteria for places at risk and what may constitute a trigger for action. Gregory Stanton's analysis of genocide involves eight stages; it is not clear at which of these stages responsibility to protect comes into play, though it seems from the four defining kinds of crimes that the trigger for an international response is likely to be evidence of actual mass killing, not merely indications that such killings are likely to occur. With respect to the criteria, for example, the 2016 list of nations at risk published by the independent Responsibility to Protect Organization includes twenty-one nations, while Gregory Stanton's 2012 report on nations where genocide is occurring lists nine. However, even taking into account the possibility of improvement in those nine nations listed by Stanton in 2012, the two lists differ significantly. Stanton lists four nations that do not appear on the Responsibility to Protect Organization's list: Somalia, Ethiopia, Afghanistan and Pakistan. War continues in Afghanistan, and arguably that war has genocidal components as well as many war crimes. Pakistan is involved in the Afghan war and has its own ethnic conflict in Baluchistan, with widespread killing. In other words, the crises listed by Stanton seem to be active in 2016, and yet they do not meet the criteria of responsibility to protect. Speaking generally, Stanton's taxonomy of genocide pays more attention to the early stages, when interventions might be highly useful. In the cases of Afghanistan and

Pakistan, one wonders whether the fact that there is an alliance of Western forces carrying out war in those areas somehow places them off limits for an international discussion of genocide or war crimes. Altogether, it seems that the experts have not agreed upon criteria, though the problem of genocide is evidently large and looming.

Responsibility to protect theory combines elements of both just war theory and just peacemaking theory, in that responsibility to protect recommends various kinds of peaceful interventions in nations that have internal troubles, with the possibility of military intervention as a last resort. This last resort is called a responsibility to react. Interestingly, the five "precautionary principles" for military intervention, according to this theory, are right intention, last resort, proportional means, reasonable prospects, and right authority (6). In this theory, right authority rests in the United Nations Security Council, which includes the major arms manufacturers and is the body that is now selecting the next Secretary General of the UN through a secretive and arguably undemocratic process, as it has done throughout the history of the UN. The right to respond (and react) theory also recommends efforts to rebuild damaged nations and to achieve justice, as does standard just war theory. It has already been noted that "right authority" may exclude the rights of people who are simply following their moral lights, as in the case of, say, the American revolutionaries. The other criteria are also familiar from just war theory, though there is a quite remarkable lack of emphasis on one of the traditional just war criteria: noncombatant immunity. Perhaps, realistically, these theorists take the view that noncombatant immunity is a fantasy. Perhaps the authors of the summary documents consider that the principle of "proportional means" necessarily encompasses traditional concerns about noncombatants. Unlike the cases of the other theories, the United Nations General Assembly adopted these principles in 2005 and created a special office to address the issue of genocide. Interventions have been made in Kenya, Libya, Central African Republic, and in other nations, with mixed results. In view of what will be discussed later concerning the evidence that nations now deliberately target civilians, some additional attention to noncombatant immunity would be valuable.

The International Coalition for the Responsibility to Protect lists eighteen nations, as of August 2016, where citizens may need international protection, including such familiar locations as the Democratic Republic of the Congo and Myanmar. Most of the nations are in Africa. Venezuela might be added to this list, given the recent reports of people unable to get food and even fresh water in that nation. The list of nations in need is praiseworthy in the sense that it includes countries such as Zimbabwe, where there is an evident need for regime change and, very likely, some prospect of a more peaceful transition than has been accomplished in South Sudan.

Critics of the responsibility to protect have pointed out that the policy is problematic because it involves infringing on national sovereignty. Moreover, it is likely to be implemented only where national sovereignty is so weak that an intervention is physically more possible. For that reason, there are unlikely to be interventions in places such as North Korea, or Venezuela, or even Zimbabwe. Regional diplomatic and economic pressures no doubt play a role in these decisions. Hence, one is not likely to see interventions in strong and stable autocratic states. Responsibility to protect is a welcome addition to the treaties that are already in place, though as the rest of this chapter explains, the mechanisms of treaties and conventions have not proved very strong. With respect to the focus of this book, limitations of responsibility to protect are that it waits for mass killing, that it does not include an emphasis on noncombatant immunity, that it does not systematically address the proliferation of weapons that make genocide easy, and that officially it depends on the decision of the UN Security Council, which is under the control of the major arms-manufacturing nations.

The general limitations of just war theories can be placed under three headings. First, they are not binding laws or treaties, even if, as in the case of the responsibility to protect doctrine, the principles have been affirmed and adopted by the UN General Assembly. They are merely philosophical guidelines, and they have seldom been systematically invoked, though national debates over wars do tend to raise questions of cost effectiveness, noncombatant casualties, nation building, mission creep, and justice. Second, while the theories are noble, there is no reason to believe that any nation, pushed to the limits of its resources, has followed the precepts of just war theory and declined to kill civilians, or to use excessive force, or to violate the principles in some other way. Third, while just peacemaking theory embodies generous ideas, it can easily be viewed as a neocolonial project to help people and movements whose cultures and ideas may not share the all the values of the major Western democracies. Some people see genuine virtues in monarchy, or in older systems of tribal governance. They do not want to have democratic systems forced upon them, and they may have little training or education about how such systems might work to their advantage.

Moreover, the just peacemaking mandate to advance human rights is perplexing because it is an American initiative. The late Glen Stassen was the son of Harold Stassen, who ran for President of the United States more times than anyone else. Glen Stassen's objective was morally edifying, though his theory is a case of "physician heal thyself," because many of the human rights for which he argued are not present in the United States itself, and until those rights are well established in the US, Americans are not in a strong position to tell other people how to make them realities. The absence of human rights in the United States of America has become a focus of public attention with the Black Lives Matter movement and the continued killings of African Americans by police and citizens who are not African American. If the United States cannot provide equal treatment for its own citizens, should it not be the case that those who want to develop just peacemaking skills and values should first perfect how to teach and secure those values in the United States?

This point is worth emphasizing because of the tendency of the United States and other Western powers to vaunt their moral superiority. Michelle Alexander's study, *The New Jim Crow*, has made a strong case for the failure of the American system of justice, where laws differentiated between the penalties for crack and powdered cocaine, where there are more prisoners than in any other nation of the world, where 40% of the prisoners are African American though that racial group is only 11% of the population, and where 97% of cases are settled by plea bargains in which a person, whether innocent or guilty, has a choice among an often inadequate system of public defenders, high-cost private legal services, and pleading guilty to a lesser charge in exchange for a smaller penalty. Many other failures of basic rights could be listed: inequality in hiring and wages among races and genders, the large percentage of Americans living below the poverty line, inadequate or excessively expensive health care, and many others.

While the nations of the world have not officially adopted either just war theory or just peacemaking theory, they have wrestled with the ideas behind these theories for centuries. Moreover, groups of nations have attempted to formulate and enact treaties that prohibit some forms of violence in war. The object of this chapter is to summarize what has been achieved through treaties—and what has not been achieved. The overall point is that while a great deal of effort has been expended to limit the damage of war, that effort has not been successful. Once the weapons are out there, they will tend to be used to their maximum potential, though perhaps some particularly odious kinds of weapons have been abandoned most of the time in most nations.

Responsibility to protect theory may or may not have the same limitations of just peacemaking theory. Worth investigating will be the extent to which this new strategy for intervention promulgates values that may be neocolonial. Is enough respect given to local ways of getting things done in a morally acceptable way?

Judith Gardam, an Australian legal scholar, has published two thorough studies of what international treaties have attempted to achieve by way of controlling war. Her two books are *Necessity, Proportionality and the Use of Force by States* and *Non-Combatant Immunity as a Norm of International Humanitarian Law*. What follows is a critical summary of her findings.

Gardam is concerned chiefly with *jus in bello*, the standards that apply during war, and with the 1977 Protocol One of the Geneva Convention. She profiles the history of just war theory, noting the work of Hugo Grotius in the late Reformation. Grotius held that wars were understood to be between states and all of their civilians, so while noncombatant immunity was a good objective, in fact everyone in every country at war could be considered a fair target. Jean-Jacques Rousseau argued that war was always between states, not individuals, implying that individuals should be spared. The Lieber Code of 1863, developed in the American Civil War, held that it was appropriate to starve enemy civilians, because all civilians were part of the enemy. International treaties began to emerge after the holocaust of the American Civil War with the first Geneva Convention of 1864. This was followed by the St. Petersburg Declaration of 1868, which aimed to prohibit exploding musket balls. The Brussels Declaration of 1874 outlawed poison, and the Hague Conference of 1899 proscribed poison gas. Obviously poison gas was widely used in World War I, and it has continued to be used, such as in the Iraqi attacks on Iran during their eight year trench war and during the Iraqi attack on Kurdish forces in the north of Iraq, as well as more recently in Syria. A follow-on Hague Regulation in 1907 attempted to refine the earlier Hague document. The Kellogg-Briand Pact of 1928 attempted to outlaw war.

In World War II, there was widespread targeting of noncombatants, including the deaths of twelve million civilians from aerial bombardments designed to destroy the morale of enemies. World War II was followed by attempts to ban specific kinds of weapons, such as land mines and lasers that could blind, though those who discussed these treaties found it difficult to work out how to apply their rules to civil wars, such as the conflict within Iraq between Kurds and the central government. A review of literature on what constitutes a bad weapon suggests that nations are chiefly concerned about publicity (Blessed). A bad weapon is one that leaves an ugly corpse. The United States has forbidden photographers to visit the base where the coffins of American troops arrive because of the power of that publicity. Networks have in turn shown the faces of each dead American soldier for years. Limits on weapons to a large extent are governed by the visible pain and deformity caused by particular weapons. Current US policy seems to be that civilian casualties are acceptable so long as they are proportional to military objectives on the ground, though how one calculates that proportionality is obscure (Gardam, 90). At the same time, the Geneva Convention of 1949 called for humane treatment of noncombatants, though the definition of "humane" also remains obscure.

Limitations on poison and poisonous gasses have not kept nations from using other forms of chemical warfare. Morocco has recently bombed Sahrawi refugee camps in Algeria with white phosphorous and napalm, and of course the United States used napalm and Agent Orange in Vietnam and continues to use depleted uranium projectiles in the Middle East, leaving battlefields strewn with fragments of radioactive material.

All of these treaties are flawed because almost all weapons are inherently disproportionate, because if the point of war is to break an opponent's will to fight, methods short of killing should be sufficient for the purpose. Presumably this is the rationale behind blockades and quarantines and other measures designed to withhold materials from an enemy. Whether these means are effective, as in the recent cases of Iraq and Iran, is not within the purview of this book.

While in the current world climate it may seem absurd to state this: killing is always excessive. It might be possible to wage war with nets to immobilize people, or gasses to make them nauseous. Police departments around the world have tasers, rubber bullets, and nets, though often officers turn instead to lethal force. The treaties are full of terms that defy definition: proportional, attack, military advantage, cumulative effect, and incident by incident. Cumulatively, the loser of any war has miscalculated the necessary amount of violence. Conversely, any side that wins a war can claim that obviously it used appropriate force, because it was enough to win.

Gardam offers as an example the US invasion of Panama, which in her opinion used disproportionate force to achieve its objective. However, as the invasion was successful, there was little international comment (Proportionality, 167). In that case, the US violated international law and its own policies. On December 20, 1989, the US invaded Panama with 25,000 troops, and several hundred Panamanians were killed. All of that to capture the corrupt President Manuel Noriega, who was taken to the United States, where he was tried and is serving a forty-year term for drug offenses (Military.com). An invasion of 25,000 troops to capture one drug baron.

Gardam points out that the British military states that decisions must always be made on the basis of information available at the time of an attack (Non-Combatant, 106). While this is a realistic standard from the perspective of soldiers under direct attack, in practice it means that the decision to kill noncombatants is one that involves very little collecting or weighing of evidence. In effect, such a standard throws all the just war and treaty criteria out the window. The situation of troops currently assigned to rotations in Iraq and Afghanistan is truly horrendous. The rules of engagement specify that a soldier may be prosecuted for committing crimes against civilians. However, that soldier may be wearing 100 or more pounds of protective gear in 120 degree Fahrenheit weather, with 90% humidity, and standing in the face of people from a different culture speaking languages he or she does not understand and using gestures that are equally incomprehensible. The soldier's situation is impossible. What kind of information does a soldier have under those circumstances, and how fair is it to second-guess a soldier under those conditions? This points to the fundamental flaw of all just war theories: they cannot work well in practice, not typically in the run-up to wars, though they might succeed there, and certainly not in the heat of warfare where accurate information is seldom available.

On another view, proportionality in combat is reduced to the principle that you do not make direct attacks on civilians alone, though in the setting of Baghdad or Kabul, where combatants may not wear uniforms, it may not be possible to discriminate between an enemy soldier and a civilian.

Moreover, these rules become cumbersome when many nations work together in alliances. Sometimes, each nation has its own rules of engagement and either participates or declines to participate in specific kinds of military actions.

Gardam points out that the San Remo Manual on International Law Applicable in Armed Conflicts at Sea even permits attacks on hospital ships (Non-Combatant, 110; ICRC.com;San Remo Manual). Not only are these various treaties vague and unenforceable, they are also utterly puzzling in their rulings.

According to Gardam, the issues faced by peace treaties and treaties to limit the use of weapons are becoming more rather than less complex. Self-defense has always been permitted. Now there are discussions of anticipatory self-defense, which of course is an aspect of the so-called "war on terror." Under the Bush Doctrine of Right to Respond, any nation theoretically has a presumptive right to invade anywhere it sees a likelihood of danger, humanitarian disaster, or a potential threat. Weapons of Mass Destruction constitute a rationale. Recent history suggests that the capacity of likely enemies to launch terrorist attacks also constitutes a rationale for invasion, bombing, or drone strikes. Under such a regime, the theoretical questions raised by just war theory and just peacemaking theory are empty. If a nation perceives a strong enough threat, whether "existential" or of some other kind, there is no need to wait and negotiate, or to frame a clear and limited objective, or to seek to use proportionate force, or to guarantee the safety of noncombatants. The strictures of the last hundred and fifty years of international agreements also become void.

Gardam points out that another limitation of all the treaties is the definition of what constitutes the time frame of a war. All calculations of noncombatant casualties face this dilemma. As has been observed several times in this book, government calculations of noncombatant deaths prefer to calculate people killed or injured immediately. Those calculations tend not to take into account downstream casualties, such as the up to 500,000 Iraqis dead or injured because of the destruction of Iraqi infrastructure, or the up to five million Africans dead as a consequence of the war started in the Congo in 1960.

Gardam's analysis of the international record is full of cautious conclusions concerning the obvious good will of those who sat down for negotiations and the clear failure of compliance with treaties, as well as the lack of an adequate international system to hold individuals or nations accountable. The depressing lack of results indicates that in war nations will do whatever it takes to win. They will use all the weapons they have made or bought. Increasingly, that means they will carry out total wars without regard to the lives of noncombatants.

From a philosophical perspective, the status of just war theory and of international covenants to control war is perplexing and also full of irony. The full irony of the situation can be appreciated by looking briefly at the differences among three closely related kinds of theories that have varying degrees of legal traction in the United States: just war theory, human subjects review standards, and animal rights standards. Human subjects review law was created after the Tuskegee syphilis study, in which a number of African American men were infected with syphilis and followed until they died, even though during the period of the study, penicillin became available and all the subjects could have been treated. Under human subjects review laws, which have been adopted around the world, experimenters must obtain informed consent for medical experiments, and the experiments themselves must meet a variety of safety standards. Human subjects review boards that include impartial scientists and members of the public, rule on whether experiments will be allowed to proceed. Animal welfare law developed in the United States after a case in which a kidnapped pet dog was found to have been purchased for a painful medical experiment. Under animal welfare law, an Institutional Animal Care and Use Committee (IACUC) must approve any experiment that uses an animal that has a spinal cord. Like human subjects review panels, IACUCs include impartial scientists and members of the public. The standards of care are highly detailed, and laboratories are inspected annually by federal inspectors who can levy fines on the spot for any shortcomings in experiments, animal housing, quality of drugs and general animal care. This author has chaired a university IACUC. What is striking about these three sets of standards—just war theory, human subjects review, and the Animal Welfare Act—is that under current law, nonhuman vertebrate animals have the highest level of protection. A group of scientists, nonscientists, and public members must agree that a specific experiment meets all the criteria that cover animal experiments. The animals, in other words, have a whole group of professional advocates. Under human subject review, a subject of an experiment can sign the consent form, and while the experiment as a whole has been approved by a human subjects review board, the members of that board are not advocates for patients in the same way as are the members of an IACUC. IACUC panels visit the animals and inspect the care. They check to see if the food and water are fresh, if temperature and humidity in living spaces are appropriate, if cages are the right sizes, if animals have toys to entertain them, and so on. Human subjects review board members are not required to visit patients or experimental subjects, though of course all experiments are monitored by experts who visit sites and collect data. Turning to just war theory, there is first of all no law that mandates that anyone make a determination that a war is just. Neither is there anyone who advocates for teenagers who sign up to join military forces, examines the standards of care in military training installations, or monitors wars. Certainly lab animals deserve all the protections they get. The point is that the system as a whole seems to be backwards: the lowest level of care is provided to those at highest risk, those who must fight wars. Subjects of medical experiments receive the next level of care, and laboratory animals have the highest level of protection because they cannot speak for themselves. At issue, of course, is whether teenagers who sign up to join military services have either appropriate judgment and maturity or appropriate information about the commitments they make.

The world has not established a working system of laws or treaties or theories to control wars.

7

Targeting Civilians

On July 1, 2016, the American government revealed that drone strikes had accidentally killed up to 166 civilians. The point of this admission was certainly to assure the public that American forces carry out "surgical" strikes and operate with extraordinary efficiency and precision. Many international watchdog groups immediately responded that the total of civilians killed by American forces was far higher. The UN Assistance Mission in Afghanistan, which requires any death to be confirmed by multiple sources, lists about 2,000 civilian deaths per year, of which about one third are committed by pro-Afghan government forces. This estimate of course includes people killed by the Afghan army itself as well as those killed by non-American soldiers. Wikipedia's heavily edited pages on this topic, using many sources, including the Iraqi Body Count project and the Iraq War Log, indicate that the number of civilian deaths in the recent past has ranged from about 66,000 to 120,000.

Alexander Downes' well-received research, presented in *Targeting Civilians in War*, published in 2008, makes a compelling case that armies of democratic states tend to target civilians, even more so than the armies of dictatorships, because the citizens of democracies easily tire of war or protest wars. Therefore democracies must produce results quickly. While there has been nothing quick about the ongoing war on terror, which has lasted over 13 years in Iraq and Afghanistan, Downes builds his case carefully.

His point can be broadened. Obviously, civilians are easier to kill because they are not armed and they are not expecting to be targets. This is what makes terrorism effective, and this is why American advocates of broad Second Amendment rights want to assure that everyone in the United States can own weapons for self-defense.

Gardam's studies show that the congeries of international treaties that have been signed to reduce killing have failed. Downes' work is compelling because he shows that not only is there insufficient concern for the lives of noncombatants, the fact is that nations deliberately target noncombatants in order to win wars quickly. This strategy is not something from the past. It is either deliberately or ineluctably part of the way that contemporary wars are waged.

In addition, Downes' work confirms another well-known fact about violence that is also supported by studies of moral choices. People care less about those who are different from themselves, or to put it bluntly, racism and religious prejudice play a major role in wars. People who are defined as barbarians have no rights. Downes' most important finding, however, is that nations appear to make strategic choices to target civilians in order to win wars quickly, and this strategic objective sometimes carries more weight than racism or xenophobia, though those forms of prejudice still play their parts. This raises a profound question: Which is worse, to view people as killable because they are Muslims, or Arabs, or Jews, or Americans, or Christians, or to view them as killable because they are just civilians whose deaths in large numbers will put political pressure on an enemy to bring an end to a war?

Downes' book is full of statistical analyses. His starting point is the conclusion that over the last three centuries, between 50% and 64% of all deaths from war have been noncombatants. Downes notes Michael Walzer's contention that anyone who works in a weapons plant has given up the right to be considered a noncombatant (14). If Walzer's point is admitted, then where does anyone draw the line about what constitutes supporting a war effort? Paying taxes? Working in a mine that produces a rare metal? Financing the operations of a weapons company? Running a railroad that transports materials or manufactured products?

Like Gardam's studies and much of the literature about noncombatants or civilians killed in wars, Downes does not include civil wars in his analysis, only wars between states. He does, however, attempt to take into account what can be called the double-effect deaths, those deaths due not to immediate strikes by bombs, for example, but also those deaths due to causes such as the destruction of water supplies, sewer plants, hospitals, and other public services. The question to raise about these estimates is the length of time studied. Does one count deaths that occur only a few days after a strike, or does one look for effects a year or more later? Most of the figures cited by government authorities for the Iraq war, for example, include only direct collateral damage: immediate deaths of civilians who were in the area of a bomb or a drone strike. International watchdog groups tend to count longer-term deaths due to injuries and to the destruction of essential public services.

For example, in the case of Iraq, up through the 2008 publication date of his book, Downes cites studies that indicate 111,000 Iraqis probably died as a consequence of destroying the Iraqi electrical grid (226). Others have estimated that sanctions against Iraq have killed 227,000, with about 60 children dying per day because of the failure of the health system, in part due to the unavailability of medical resources (231). The British medical publication *Lancet* estimated 665,000 as the number of excess deaths caused by the war as of 2006 (235). Iraq Body Count, however, offered a total of 12,829 civilian deaths (235), though the Iraq Body Count data currently available on the web indicate far higher totals of deaths for that period. Downes concludes that the *Lancet* estimate is probably high, though his reason is that most Iraqi deaths are caused not by outside troops, but rather by Iraqis themselves, as in the case of car bombings. Still, if these are excess deaths caused by the state of war that began with the destabilizing of Iraq, then the *Lancet* estimate may be more correct. For Downes' purpose, the question is whether outside forces target civilians, though civilians targeted by internal terrorist groups would seem to meet the necessary criteria. It doesn't matter which army kills civilians; it matters that civilians are targeted and killed. Overall, Downes finds that the United States is likely to target civilians if it becomes desperate, in the sense that the military must show results to satisfy citizens and the political system at home. A contributing factor is that in a street war, the US loses its technological advantages. The boots on the ground are vulnerable, far more vulnerable than the pilots of the bombers or the drivers of long-distance drones.

It should be emphasized here that Downes draws a distinction between those Iraqis killed by foreign troops and those Iraqis killed by fellow citizens. War and civil war often go together. This is clearly the case in Syria during the last five years. It is true anywhere a state of war liberates competing parties to carry out their own vengeance and their own attempts to seize power. It seems illegitimate to be so punctilious about trying to define the differences between an Iraqi civilian killed accidentally or deliberately by an Allied strike and an Iraqi civilian killed by an Iraqi who belongs to another Islamic sect. All of the deaths are due to the destabilization of the nation and to the ongoing state of general war. When distinctions and definitions of this kind are used to minimize the number of deaths in a particular conflict, that strategy of redefining reality is wrong.

Downes reaches the shocking conclusion that democracies are 83% more likely to target civilians than autocracies. According to him, the primary motivation for mass killing is to get wars done quickly (48). Downes would like to conclude that there has been less mass killing of civilians since World War II, or at least since Vietnam. However, the number of civilian deaths in Iraq undermines that argument and supports the conclusion that civilians are still routinely targeted. Downes also analyzed differences between what he defined as "wars of attrition" compared to "wars of annexation" compared to other wars, presumably defensive wars. His conclusion is that compared to other kinds of wars, wars of attrition kill 7.5 times as many civilians and wars of annexation kill 12 times as many civilians. A difficulty with applying these definitions, however, is to determine, in the chaos of war and of "mission creep" just what are the differences among these kinds of wars.

The ongoing war in Iraq could be called a war of annexation if one focuses on the motivation of controlling oil resources. Annexation need not be direct political control of a nation if a power succeeds in establishing indirect political control with substantial economic control of key natural resources and industries. The history of postcolonial Africa is full of situations in which European nations control parts of African nations without directly annexing territory in the traditional sense of direct conquest and occupation. Iraq is a war of attrition in the sense that the Kurd vs. Sunni vs. Shiite battle looks very much like an ongoing war of attrition among groups that have been in conflict since the early days of Islam. Iraq is a defensive war insofar as one credits the view that this "war on terror" serves to defend the territory of the United States from invasion by terrorists. It is again a war of attrition if one sees it from the perspective of an Iranian strategist hoping to reduce the power of Sunni forces in Iraq or elsewhere. It is also a war of attrition if one takes the perspective that the war on terror is a war against fundamentalist Islam, because there is no way of calculating the extent of such a war, except to observe that more violence, unemployment, and chaos radicalizes more Muslims, and in the end there are between 1.6 and 1.8 billion Muslims in the world. From the standpoint of some who carry out the war, killing Muslim enemies may be attrition; from the standpoint of others, this is a war of addition, because more Muslims are induced to join. It seems at times as if some leaders in the United States do think in terms of a total war between the West (whatever that is, exactly) and the Muslim world. Paul Nehlen, a candidate for the national House of Representatives in the American state of Wisconsin proposed in August 2016 that all Muslims be expelled from the United States.

Downes concludes further that because of political pressure to get the job done, democracies engage in mass killing 57% of the time in wars of attrition compared to non-democracies, which engage in mass killing only 15% of the time, because autocracies do not need to consider the voices of their publics. These analyses leave out another consideration, however: the extent to which nations target soldiers who have dropped their weapons or surrendered and have therefore become noncombatants at least in some sense. This is an important factor, once again, in Iraq, because the air campaign in Operation Desert Storm appears to have killed between 10,000 and 12,000 Iraqi troops, many of whom had left their equipment and were fleeing back toward Baghdad.

Downes' conclusions are based on statistical analyses of the relationship between civilian and military deaths. He makes a general inference that where civilian deaths are high, it is likely that those civilians have been targeted. He compares the number of civilians killed by democracies and by totalitarian governments to reach his general conclusions. He does not present documentary evidence in the form of memos written by generals or presidents stating their intention to kill noncombatants in order to get wars finished. Here, as with the general thesis of this book, the issue is whether it is fair to conclude that a system has a specific intent if in fact it can be shown that a system routinely produces a specific and predictable effect. Downes concludes that civilians are targeted when the statistics show that in fact civilians are killed in larger numbers.

A brief examination of just one of the world's many long-lasting wars indicates just how difficult it is to define war, war between states, civil war, genocide, noncombatant casualties, civilian casualties, and nearly any other term that scholars such as Gardam and Downes employ, in good conscience, to circumscribe and measure the casualties of war.

By 1880, most of Africa had been carved into European colonies under the control of Britain, France, Germany, Portugal, and Spain. The biggest chunk of Africa left over was the former Kongo empire, the land west of the great African lakes, north of Portuguese Angola, and south of the French territory of the Congo. Rather than go to war over this land that had not been seized by a European power, the great powers met in Berlin during 1884 and 1885 and came to the conclusion that the safest way to avoid a war was to give the area to a minor European state, or rather to its king as his personal property. Belgian King Leopold mined the Congo Free State for as much income as it could produce.

So began one of the darker episodes in nineteenth-century colonial history. So also begins a story that is far from over and that is likely to make headlines in the future. South of the territory granted to the King of Belgium lay yet another stretch of land that had not been seized by any European power. What came next served as the foundation for Joseph Conrad's novella *Heart of Darkness*. Conrad's famous tale, which ends with the words, "the horror, the horror," is actually far tamer than the reality. Both the British and the Belgians sent expeditions into the unclaimed land to reach an agreement with the local king. The King of Belgium hired a British lieutenant to lead the Belgian expedition. Lieutenant Stairs and his Belgian party reached the territory before the British expedition. He met with the King of the Garanganze people to ask if he would bring his territory under Belgian administration. The King said no, and the next day Stairs came back for a second visit, during which either he or one of his party emptied his revolver into the king's body and cut off the king's head with a machete. These ugly details are important because of the subsequent history.

The King of the Garanganze himself lived in a compound surrounded by the staked heads of his enemies and those of criminals, like the compound in which Conrad's Kurtz is found on the banks of the Congo River. Lieutenant Stairs publicly proclaimed the Belgian King's rule of the area by jamming the local king's head onto a tall stake and displaying it outside the King's residence

The subsequent Belgian colonial rule of the Congo represented the nadir of European colonial history. The American poet Vachel Lindsay wrote a famous poem, *The Congo*, that described the brutality of the regime, such as the practice of rubber plantation overseers who told crew bosses to come back from a day's work with baskets full of rubber sap or baskets full of the amputated hands and feet of laborers who had come up short. Adam Hochschild's recent history of Leopold's private reign of the Congo Free State, reviewed by Michiko Kakutani in the *The New York Times*, summarizes the totality of the violence. Belgian troops stole food and raided crops, whipped native people to death, worked them to death in rubber plantations, and created conditions that led to millions of deaths by starvation and disease. It has been estimated that between 8 and 10 million Congolese died in the period between 1885 and 1908, which was about half of the population.

In 1960, when Belgium chose to liberate the Congo, the King Baudouin of Belgium traveled to Leopoldville, the capital, to participate in the ceremonial transfer of power to the new African government, which was led by the recently elected Prime Minister Patrice Lumumba. Given the well-known, violent colonial history of the Congo, no one should have been shocked that Lumumba, as he accepted the leadership of the new nation, said that the Belgian colonial rule had been harsh. Lumumba asked for assistance from the West to build a nation, and then he unwisely threatened to bring in Soviet advisors if Western aid was not forthcoming. The King of Belgium was insulted by being told publicly what he must have known. Lumumba may have been rash and impolitic. He had the courage to do what many oppressed peoples and survivors yearn to do: to speak truth to power, to speak about the horror, to ask to be heard, to ask for help. Would it have been impossible in that moment for Western powers to accept responsibility, as just peacemaking theory recommends, and as just war theory also recommends in its requirement that nations repair what they have damaged? Rumor suggests that President Eisenhower, hearing about Lumumba's speech, said he was a dead man.

Shortly after Lumumba took power, the CIA worked to bring an end to his government. Lumumba had brought in Soviet advisors, as he had promised he would do if he received no Western help. Lumumba fled his capital and was captured, tortured, hogtied, and flown south in the belly of a four-engine prop plane to the newly established Republic of Katanga, a breakaway state that included a valuable mining region. Once Lumumba arrived in Elisabethville, now Lubumbashi, Katanga, there is little clarity about what happened.

What Lieutenant Stairs had seized at the end of the nineteenth century turned out to be one of the richest mineral lodes in the world. When the stardust that formed the earth coalesced, by some freak of chance one half of the planet's known uranium landed in a single location. The lode was so rich that while mines of less than 1% uranium are considered rich elsewhere in the world, the lode in the Congo's province of Katanga contained ore that was on average 65% pure uranium oxide. The region also contained

Targeting Civilians

vast reserves of copper, cadmium, and other industrially valuable metals. Before World War II, the Belgian manager in charge of the uranium mine at Shinkolobwe, Katanga, was concerned enough about the fate of the ore that he sent large shipments to New York City, where it lay in a warehouse and was later used to build the first atomic bombs. The Shinkolobwe mine was not a resource that could fall under Soviet control. Belgian mining interests also worked to maintain control over the other mineral resources. The Republic of Katanga was ruled by the flamboyant Moise Tshombe, who had led a breakaway movement, and by his associate Godefroid Munongo, his minister of information. Both men served in many roles. Tshombe was briefly president of the entire Congo before he in turn was deposed. Godefroid Munongo was the grandson of Msiri, the King of the Garanganze people who had been murdered by Lieutenant Stairs, and Godefroid, in turn later became the King of the Garanganze. Within African nations, it is common for national or federal governments to recognize traditional kingships and other political structures. Munongo had said publicly that if the Belgians did not have the courage to kill Lumumba, he did. According to some accounts, Lumumba was shot by former Belgian troops who worked as mercenaries for the Katangese government. On another account, Lumumba was tied to a tree and shot by a firing squad of Belgian troops. On yet another account, Godefroid Munongo personally tortured and then hacked Lumumba to death with a machete, similar to the way that his grandfather's body was treated, though no one placed Lumumba's head on a stake for public viewing. What was left of his body was either burned, or cut up and dumped in battery acid, or both before the remains were buried.

United Nations peacekeeping forces were sent to Katanga in an effort to bring an end to a multi-party war that soon broke out. The Katangese government fought the Congolese army, which was trying to bring an end to the secession. The Katangese forces may also have been carrying out genocide against the Baluba people, one of the important local tribes. In terms of the categories and definitions mobilized by scholars such as Gardam and Downes, what was going on in the Congo was a great power decision to defy the peace efforts of the Secretary General of the United Nations and support a secessionist government to secure mineral resources, while other secessions took place, while a civil war or tribal war developed on the ground, and while eventually other powers stepped in, including Che Guevara, who arrived on the banks of Lake Tanganyika to offer support to the Simba rebels who were active in the center and east of the Republic of the Congo. Real war is far messier than any of the definitions.

What happened next is still the subject of debate, up through a report issued by a special commission appointed by the Secretary General of the United Nations, Ban Ki Moon, in 2015, and the possibility that a further special investigation will be called for based on information revealed in 2016. The issue was what the Western powers were going to do to preserve control over the largest deposit of uranium in the world at the height of the Cold War, when at the same time the Secretary General of the United Nations had clearly staked out a position of international leadership and had also berated both the West and the Communist powers for their conduct. Susan Williams' book, *Who Killed Hammarskjold?*, led to the new UN inquiry that made its report at the end of 2015, one of several that have been carried out since the death of Secretary General Dag Hammarskjold in a plane crash in 1961. Hammarskjold was on his fourth mission to the Congo to try to negotiate a peace deal and re-unify the Congo, which was torn by at least one, perhaps two, secessionist governments and at least another uprising. Key evidence that led to the latest, completed UN inquiry included a statement by a former CIA officer posted to a listening station in Cyprus that he was awakened late at night to listen to the radio transmission from the plane that shot down the Secretary General. That most recent UN panel concluded that there was abundant evidence that the death of the Secretary General was not an accident, but that without further data and supporting witnesses, including the willingness of the United States, Britain, and France to make specific classified records available to investigators, no further progress could be made toward the truth. However, on August 1, 2016, *Foreign Policy* issued an exclusive report that still more evidence had emerged, implicating the American CIA and a South African intelligence agency in a plot, with the UK and a Belgian mining company, to eliminate Hammarskjold. Secretary General Ban Ki Moon asked for yet another investigation. If the United States, Britain, and France agreed, either alone or with the Belgian government and perhaps elements of the South African government and/or white activists in British African colonies, to kill the Secretary General of the United Nations in order to bring an end to international peace negotiations, there are no criteria of any just war, just peacemaking, right to respond, or responsibility to protect theory that fit the situation, although we have seen other instances that are similar in their lack of respect for all standards. The United States, Britain, and its allies went to war in Iraq based on fabricated evidence that was presented to the United Nations. The British government in July 2016 issued a report about the errors of Prime Minister Blair, and groups are calling for a similar inquiry into the actions of President George W. Bush in the United States. In 1961, there was no effort to fabricate a rationale. The United Nations already had a peacekeeping force on the ground, but the objectives of the Secretary General were apparently not to the liking of the powers that needed to control the mineral resources. As Susan Williams points out, there were also white leaders in what were then Northern and Southern Rhodesia (now Zambia and Zimbabwe) who were not interested in having those colonies liberated and placed under Black African rule. So the Secretary General was killed. "They got him," is what former President Truman is rumored to have said. Neither is it clear how killing the Secretary General improved the bargaining positions of those who may have ordered the killing, since the next Secretary General helped to bring an end to the Katangese succession, and the corrupt pro-Western government that was installed in the Congo was arguably neither better nor worse than any that might have been installed if Hammarskjold had lived.

On his fourth flight into the Congo, Dag Hammarskjold planned to land not in Katanga, but at Ndola, an airport inside what was then Northern Rhodesia. His plane crashed in a rainstorm. The American consul in Katanga expressed the view that the experienced Swedish pilot had mistaken Ndola, Angola, for Ndola, Northern Rhodesia, and had misjudged his altitude. That Angolan town was over a thousand miles further west. The story is not credible. The CIA officer's testimony about hearing the radio transmission from the plane that shot down the Secretary General, which was not adequately confirmed by additional witnesses, suggested strongly that the US government had prior knowledge of what would happen. A US Air Force electronics plane was on the ground at Ndola, Northern Rhodesia, with its engines running. It was rumored that the death of another African leader had been due to electronic interference with his plane's navigation equipment. White Rhodesian leaders had their own reasons to dislike Hammarskjold. Before his plane attempted a landing, the airport authorities turned off the landing beacons, contrary to all normal practice in times of a delayed flight. The sole survivor, Sergeant Harold Julien, the American chief of security, said the plane had been shot down. Local African people on the ground testified they had seen a pursuit plane. The Katangese had more than one Czech fighter-trainer with appropriate armament, though others suggested the pursuit plane was an old P-38. Hammarskjold was lionized after his death, remembered as a peacemaker, granted the only posthumous Nobel Peace Prize, and praised for the volume of Christian reflections he left behind, *Markings*, which was for a time a bestseller.

After Hammarskjold's death, the Western powers tried various leaders for a reunified Congo until they found Joseph Mobuto, who ruled as Mobutu Sese Soko. The task of resolving the civil war temporarily, however, required another extraordinary intervention. Once considered the CIA's most successful war, the defeat of the Simba rebellion in the eastern Congo involved the creation of an independent air force, including one WWII bomber, and the hiring of a notorious group of white mercenaries to do battle with the local fighters, who were tenuously supported by Che Guevara for a time, though all of his communications were intercepted by a US Navy ship off the coast of East Africa, and Che seems to have failed to reach an understanding with the local rebels. On the American side, the CIA's lead mercenary, Mike Hoare, hired Cuban American veterans of the Bay of Pigs operation to fight Che Guevara and the African rebels. The picture here is a familiar one of major nations interfering in the affairs of smaller sovereign nations without much concern for international law, international treaties, or anything but often-obscure goals. The CIA war against the Simba rebellion does not look so successful now, in view of the fact that the war has continued in one form or another since 1960—for a period of fifty-eight years and counting. Histories of these wars, including body counts published by various specialists, often tend to parse the war as a sequence of separate engagements, though they run so seamlessly that it seems false to call the tragedy of the Congo anything but a perpetual war brought about by the failure of the process of granting freedom to a colony. This so-called World War of Africa may have killed as many as five million people by now, and counting. Caldwell et al. estimate 2.5 million dead between 1998 and 2001 alone, of which only 6% were battlefield deaths, and the other 94% various kinds of noncombatant deaths. Depending on one's view, this ongoing war includes Joseph Kony's Lord's Army in Uganda, whose beliefs about being safe from bullets echo those of the earlier Simba fighters. The war also could include the two episodes of genocide in Rwanda between the Hutu and the Tutsi and, as of 2016, the emerging difficulties in Burundi. The Congo and its surrounding nations are still not stable. The war is not over.

There are many differences between the Congo and Oman. One is that the character of leaders matters. Sultan Qaboos could have replaced his father, moved to Switzerland, and directed all the revenues of his desert nation to his own bank accounts. Instead, he stayed in his nation and led a renaissance that has lasted more than 40 years. Mobutu Sese Soko skimmed the wealth of the Congo and sent it to Swiss banks. He also failed to develop the nation he led. The character of international advisors matters too. Sultan Qaboos had many local and international advisors and a clear plan of action. It is not clear what criteria, other than loyalty to the West, Mobutu satisfied, nor what advice he sought or received, or whether the task in the Congo under any leadership was far greater than the task in relatively small and homogeneous Oman.

In 1992, Godefroid Munongo, who may have personally killed Patrice Lumumba and who in the 90s held his grandfather's position as King of the Garanganze, tired of answering questions about what had happened in the early years of the conflict. He called a news conference in which he promised to tell the whole truth. Two hours before the event was to start, he died suddenly of a heart attack. His relatives have said he was poisoned. At the root of this story is a conviction on the part of many national leaders that a quick, violent act can solve a potential problem, in this case the possibility that the Soviet Union might gain control of essential resources, including most of the world's uranium.

More important, perhaps, is what has happened to the uranium mine over which this war may have started. Its openings were filled with concrete, under the direction of American engineers. Then the mine area was flooded with water. Its location was wiped off maps. The area itself was fenced. However, artisanal miners have been working the area, carrying ore out for sale to whomever pays the price. Meanwhile, the Chinese government has invested in rebuilding the railroad from Luanda, Angola, on the Atlantic coast, to Katanga. The railroad had fallen into disrepair during the Angolan revolution. Is it likely that with good foresight and a need to reduce reliance on fossil fuel, the Chinese are preparing to reopen the largest supply of nuclear fuel in the world? The Shinkolobwe mine and its history are the topics of Susan Williams' newest book, *Spies in the Congo*.

It beggars belief that in 1960, during the heat of the Cold War, Western powers could participate in the murder of the Secretary General of the United Nations, the assassination of the first elected leader of the Congo, and the initiation of a war that still continues, all of that to preserve control of mines, including the largest uranium mine on the planet, and then walk away from that resource and possibly leave it to China. The issue is not whether it is good or bad for China to make use of the resource, if that is the intention of the Chinese. The issue is, rather, that so many have died for a prize that in the end was apparently cast away, and that no better outcome could have been secured by such means as working with Prime Minister Lumumba and his government—or any successor government—to make an economic and political success of the new Republic of the Congo.

According to Caldwell's sources, in 2010 the still unsuccessful UN mission to stabilize the Congo involved 19,008 personnel (199). In that same fiscal year, the total cost of UN peacekeeping missions was $7.62 billion (199). When one totals the amounts of money involved in both legal and illegal weapons sales, and the generally incalculable amounts of lost production, destruction of infrastructure, and recovery, one finds that the cost of war and the cost of targeting civilians is remarkably high. Caldwell's sources, cited earlier, indicate that only 6% of those who died in the Congo were soldiers. Of course this is a situation that challenges Downes' reasoning. It may be difficult to assert that any Congolese government in the past half-century has deliberately targeted civilians, in this civil war, in order to bring about a quick end to a war. The country has not been democratic. There has been no victory in the war and not much indication of strategy or planning. It is rather a situation in which chaos and murder continue in the absence of government.

When Alexander Downes considers the circumstances in which nations may target civilians to win wars quickly, his models have no application to the situation in the Congo. Dag Hammaskjold was a civilian. The one million or five million Congolese and people of other nationalities have mostly been civilians. They have not always been the victims of organized armed forces. Instead, they have been killed by roving bands of government soldiers, revolutionaries or separatist groups, by members of other communities or tribes, and by starvation and illness. There is nothing strategic or tactical about this war. It is an ongoing, self-fueled holocaust allowed to happen because of an absence of investment and an absence of central government authority. What is common to this war and to the kinds of wars that Gardam and Downes do consider is the belief that weapons and violence can be solutions.

Ethicists often write about direct and indirect effects of actions. The immediate death of a noncombatant is a primary effect; deaths due to starvation or lack of resources over some short period after an attack are secondary effects. Discussions of just war often founder when it comes to agreeing on how long effects should be measured. Have the allies in Iraq killed a relatively small number of soldiers, or a middling number of soldiers and civilians in the hours or days following attacks, or are all the people who have died because of failed water and other systems to be counted—a number that may reach half a million after the initial attacks on Baghdad? Those longer effects are the tertiary consequences of a war. In the case of the fifty-plus year World War of Africa centered on the Democratic Republic of the Congo, most of the casualties have been civilians, and they have died because of raids, episodes of genocide, actual military campaigns, and the effects of those campaigns. To repeat the count, the total number of dead has been estimated to be between one and five million, and counting.

When Downes writes about targeting civilians, he means the deliberate or perhaps somewhat thoughtless decision to kill civilians in order to bring a war to an end more quickly. What language best describes a situation like the Congo, where the motivations of each local campaign differ, where the initial motivation of the Western powers was to protect mineral resources, and where civilians are not so much targeted for any specific strategic reason but rather simply not taken into account? Fire bombing Tokyo or Dresden to bring an end to World War II, knowing that tens of thousands of civilians will die, is different from destabilizing a former colony and precipitating a multi-generation period of chaos. And yet it seems that those who destabilize nations should have known what they were doing; should have studied the ethnic, religious and political forces at work; and should be considered accountable for what they precipitate. In other words, if nations initiate wars of this kind repeatedly, and those who begin the wars have every reason to understand the likelihood of the slaughter that may follow, then the leaders who begin those wars should be judged to have *chosen* to target civilians. While there is evidence that Western nations have sometimes acted in gross ignorance of such matters as the sectarian divisions within Islam, that ignorance is culpable. Thoughtless targeting or casual targeting, or paying no heed to consequences is another kind of targeting of civilians and noncombatants.

However the killing comes about, Downes makes a strong case that the idea of noncombatant immunity has been in large measure replaced by the strategy of targeting civilians in order to win wars.

8

Our Better Angels?

Stephen Pinker's thesis in *The Better Angels of our Nature* is, to state it roughly, that the amount of violence has decreased in the world, that we are for the most part in a period of peace, and that we have the progressive ideas of the European Enlightenment to thank for our good fortune. Though Pinker's book has been widely critiqued, his ideas deserve at least to be noticed here because they run counter to the thesis of this book: that our situation is dangerous and in need of immediate remediation because the level of violence in the world is extreme and due to an important extent to the high availability of weapons, to ordinary weapons of local and direct destruction as well as to the availability of weapons of other kinds. Moreover, the availability of those weapons and the profits to be made manufacturing and selling them have predisposed nations to engage in war rather than in democratic processes of dialogue, deliberation, and long-term problem solving aimed at producing lasting peace.

Taking a longer view than Pinker does, one can observe that this planet has been around for about 4.5 billion years. Life on this planet may have begun to develop as early as 3.5 billion years ago, following a chemical process first sketched by the famous experiment of Harold Urey and Stanley Miller. The details of early evolution are not at all clear, nor is the age of our own modest species. We seem to have left Africa about 100,000 years ago, and then again perhaps 50,000 years ago. The forebears of the Sentinelese may have been part of that second trek out of Africa, and they have probably lived in isolation on their island for 40,000 years without leaving much of a footprint, carbon or otherwise. Written human language seems to be about

Our Better Angels?

5,000 years old. *The Epic of Gilgamesh*, written in Sumerian, appears to be among our earliest literary works, and its portrayal of women is utterly barbaric, leaving little doubt about how long the war against women has been going on. Systematic, dialectical, and logical reasoning appears perhaps for the first time in the work of the pre-Socratic philosopher Parmenides, and if his extraordinary writings are viewed as a statement about ethics rather than a statement about the physical nature of the universe, his point is that we are all one. It is Rodney King's point: "Why can't we all get along?" King was the Los Angeles African American severely beaten by the local police in a widely publicized case of police violence in March 1991.

Only since the European Enlightenment do we seem to have possessed the mathematical tools to resolve Zeno's paradox of motion and to calculate the relationships between two processes that are simultaneously changing. In simpler language, Calculus and differential equations date to the Enlightenment. Our model of the atom is barely a century old, and the periodic table of the elements not much older. Only in the last two generations has our species developed an understanding of the forces inside the atom, and we have learned how to build nuclear weapons that can destroy all life. We have also, insensibly, to use a word favored by Edward Gibbon in his *Decline and Fall of the Roman Empire*, loosed forces that are warming the entire planet and that may lead to catastrophic climatic changes. What is notable about this tale is how young we are as a species, for how little time we have had the capacity to write down ideas, and how quickly we have turned our capacity to calculate and to reason into the ability to destroy the fragile planet on which we ride. Given our present peril, we have little of which to be proud. As Ecclesiastes wrote (1:18), "In much knowledge is much grief, and he who increases knowledge increases sorrow." As a species, it is a truism to observe that our technological progress has far outrun our moral capacity.

Pinker's case for the decrease in global violence is based on a variety of estimates of the numbers of dead through recorded history. The foundation of this book is Joseph Popper's thought that any single human life is worth more than the aggregate of human art and science. On that basis, or on any other theory that places a high value on human lives, it is not acceptable to claim that global conditions have improved because it is possible to draw graphs that show a relative decline in deaths over time. If each life has either an infinite value or a very high and indeterminate value, then it is not possible to measure the meaning of death simply by counting corpses.

Quite apart from this critical point, Pinker's estimates can be questioned, as he has a tendency to prefer numbers that fit his case. Examining the catastrophic ongoing war in the Congo, for example, he cites one lower estimate of deaths and accepts it without assigning any reason other than the fact that that estimate is lower than others assembled by equally reputable groups (319). According to the report he prefers, about a million have died in the various Congolese wars; according to other estimates that are widely quoted, such as one published in *The Lancet*, the British medical publication, about 5.4 million have died. Pinker later notes that the same journal published an estimate of 600,000 dead in Iraq, which contrasts with his more modest and favored estimate of 90,000 deaths.

Pinker chooses to explain human violence by drawing on the views of Hobbes and Darwin. To give Pinker credit, he sees pacifism as a goal, and he offers a frank assessment of the limits of pacifism. There must be some level of force or threat to keep people in line. Konrad Lorenz's studies of animal behavior provide a more scientifically grounded view of the uses of violence than do catchphrases adopted from Hobbes (nasty, brutish, short) or Darwin (survival of the fittest). Lorenz's studies of animals showed how controlled violence serves to define communities and their behavior. What Lorenz's work does not explain is the kind of mass violence of which humans are capable, particularly when they are provided with both inducements and the weapons necessary for the task.

Pinker's primary point, that violence has decreased, is supported by a graph that shows the percentage of deaths due to war based on archaeological, anthropological, and historical studies going back as far as 17,000 years. Whatever the accuracy of these figures, the fact that the percentage has declined recently must be gauged against the rapid increase in human population. So that a lower percentage does not necessarily mean fewer deaths, even if it is morally permissible to make one to one comparisons of the value of lives or deaths, which it is not. Pinker admits that the great period of peace following World War II, which has in any case lasted only two generations, has been interrupted by two "counter currents" due to new wars after 1960 and the related phenomenon of war in developing states after many nations were freed from their colonial master states (56, 83). What weakens his analysis is the difficulty of separating civil wars from genocide, and either of those from terrorism, and the further difficulty of determining when a war is "new" or "post-colonial" rather than a new outbreak of ethnic or religious conflict that has existed for millennia. Consider

Iraq as an example. The Bible and other early sources depict a series of wars in the Middle East long before Christianity and Islam emerged. Does one consider the current conflict between Sunni and Shiite, Arab and Iranian, to be a new war or a postcolonial war? Is it a war that started before Muhammad? Or one that started in the generation after his death with the division of Islam? Or is it a war due to the curious carving up of the Ottoman Empire after World War I, or a war due to the interference of the United States in Iran after World War II? Or does one set the starting date at some other time for a different reason or reasons?

When Pinker claims that colonial wars "no longer exist," one must ask what defines a colonial relationship. In African nations such as Nigeria, which has the largest population of any African nation, the power exercised by oil companies on the national economy in general and on the local power structure of the oil-rich coastal areas is so great that the local rebellions against both the central government and the oil companies look very much like colonial wars. What about the continuing conflicts in Tibet, the Congo, and East Timor? When Pinker observes that war is now a poor nation phenomenon (305), has it not often been the case that wars have been carried out by proxy in territories with limited or weak governance? Besides, when wars are carried out using weapons that are supplied by rich nations and rich manufacturers, would it not be equally correct to say that wars are now a rich nation phenomenon, in the sense that while wars may take place on the territory of poorer nations, they are funded by the gifts, sales, and often the economic agendas of rich nations? Moreover, for several reasons it feels tautological to say that war is a poor nation phenomenon. Poverty and domestic conflict tend to precede war and civil war. In 2016, the situation in Venezuela became increasingly dire. Food was not available in grocery stores; other basic commodities such as soap and toilet paper have been difficult to get for years; the army protects stores that sell bread. This is a situation ripe for civil war. Wars often begin where there have been previous wars that have left economic and social structures in shambles. As war proceeds, it always impoverishes nations, bringing their economies to a halt, leaving them with generations of work to re-establish infrastructure and economic institutions, and reducing the human capital necessary for making nations rich.

Pinker argues that civil wars, genocide, and terrorism are generally in decline (297). This would imply that the underlying ethnic and historical conflicts among peoples are declining. One would therefore expect to see across the world a marked decline in racial profiling, ethnic nationalism, religious conflict, and other evidence of prejudice and insularity. Given the racism that has emerged in both Europe and the United States as a result of the Syrian refugee crisis and the immigration of Muslims into the Western World, as well as the continuing racial strife in the United States, to cite just one prominent example—Black Lives Matter—it is hard to take Pinker seriously. In 2016, the Republican candidate for President of the United States won votes by promising to build a wall between the United States and Mexico and by excluding Muslims or perhaps all people who live in nations that have been touched by terrorism. Candidate Paul Nehlen, who did not win his primary campaign to run for the United States Senate, suggested that it might be good to proscribe members of religions in addition to Islam from entering the United States. It is not clear what Donald Trump has in mind in his plans to exclude people who live in nations impacted by terror, though on the broadest definition, as illustrated in the July 24, 2016, issue of the *New York Times*, such a policy of exclusion might prevent most of the people of Europe from entering the United States, as well as most people from Africa, Asia and Arabia. Further, if Pinker were correct, one might expect to see less investment in weapons. Certainly the military-industrial complex might continue to build and sell weapons that are never going to be needed. Still, there is the possibility that if peace and harmony were visibly breaking out all over, those who run weapons companies might be induced by capitalist motives to begin producing goods more attractive to that brave new world. Finally, if Pinker were correct, then one would expect to see changes in major drivers of violence, such as poverty, desertification, the excess number of males in many nations, and other foundational causes of conflict.

Taking a longer view, if Pinker were correct, one would expect to see the civilizations of the world adopting some successful and widely understood method for stopping cycles of violence. Aeschylus, in the three plays called *The Oresteia*, proposed that vengeance could be transformed into kindly and productive forces. Sometime later, Jesus of Nazareth proposed the idea of forgiveness, which Hannah Arendt called one of the two most important ideas in human history, along with the idea of promising, or making contracts and pledges that extend into the future. Neither of these ideas, psychological transformation of violent impulses into creativity or understanding the power of forgiving, has been systematically adopted and put into practice. As ideas, they have been broadly criticized as unrealistic. Western civilization does not have an effective mechanism for comprehending, transforming, and transcending its violence. We know how to deny and to forget for a time, but we have not managed to evolve a way to heal and to put an end to cycles of ethnic and community violence. Without such a transformation, it is hard to credit any suggestion that war is decreasing or is likely to decrease, which is why it is critical to reduce access to weapons.

Or, to cite an example both more down to earth and highly practical, if tensions were decreasing, there would be fewer outbreaks of identity politics, though recent elections in the United Kingdom, the United States, Hungary, France, Poland, and other nations indicate a rise in ethnic discrimination.

Pinker is correct that there has been a rights revolution. Starting with the Enlightenment, at least in the West and in some areas of the rest of the world, there has been increased attention to, and increased political and legal rights for, poor men, slaves, minorities, children, women, sexual minorities, and prisoners. The various political revolutions of the eighteenth through twentieth centuries, the abolitionist movement, the child welfare movement, the women's suffrage movement, the Civil Rights movement, the gay rights movement, and others have had important effects. What is less clear is the depth of these changes. In other words, one can point to liberation movements, new laws, and evidence of new social arrangements. At the same time, there may be more slaves in the world today than at any other time in history, the United States imprisons more people and a higher percentage of people than any other nation, and most of those prisoners are people of color. Women in the United States and elsewhere continue to earn substantially less than men, and there is abundant evidence across the world that these two- and three-hundred-year-old liberation movements have not overwhelmed and changed traditional systems of values. In fact, there are nations in Africa and Asia that have passed new and more severe codes against homosexuality, for example, and there are strong forces at work aiming to reverse many of the changes stimulated by those liberation movements. Pinker writes as if the sometimes liberal West is the entire world.

Critics of Pinker's book have also been quick to point out his strong Western and intellectual bias. He makes the case that the great ideas of the European Enlightenment are responsible for the amelioration of world conditions and the reduction in violence and war. While it is difficult to deny some causal relationship between the works of Montaigne, Locke, Kant, Rousseau, and hundreds of others on social and political history, Tolstoy's central question in *War and Peace* is still valid. Just what is responsible for historical movements? How many French people in the Revolution or the Napoleonic period were literate and how many had read Voltaire or Rousseau? To what extent were their ideas, or those of other political theorists such as Saint-Simon, responsible for changes in Europe? Tolstoy broadens his inquiry to ask how much of history can be attributed to the decisions of generals, or politicians, or diplomats, or scientists, or to the thoughts or instincts of hundreds of thousands of men who decide for no particular reason to march from Paris to Moscow and then from Moscow into the Russian winter where most of them died. Tolstoy's own answer is false. If one can show that no single one of these forces makes history, it does not follow, as he reasons, that none of them make history, and that therefore history is the result of fate or of divine action. Probably all of these forces make history together. Still, Tolstoy is right to be skeptical about the extent to which the publications of philosophers alone are responsible for history or, in the case of Pinker's argument, for the reduction in casualties due to war.

As others have also observed, Pinker gives no credit to the thinkers and leaders of other cultures, particularly non-Western cultures. Caral survived for a thousand years, apparently without war. The people of Caral had no access to Western Enlightenment ideas, and we have no idea what they thought. Asoka in India stopped conquest and established a peaceful Buddhist kingdom that lasted for two hundred years. Yes, it failed, and perhaps that case shows that pacifism alone is not enough. Still, two hundred years is a good record of survival for a largely peaceful kingdom. The Islamic tradition includes many pacifistic groups, including some Sufis, the Druze, and the Amadiyyah in Pakistan. Confucius' proposals for structuring China were in the end a successful method for tempering civil war and creating a strong monarchy with a sophisticated civil service and an ethos of duty to family and nation. Mo Tzu at the same time proposed that Chinese towns behave like Switzerland: be peaceful and so well defended that no one would want to attack. No doubt there are many more examples of powerful and long-lasting non-Western intellectual and political traditions that worked to establish peace.

The burden of Pinker's book is to suggest that the trend toward peace will continue, with occasional but small reverses. What a review of both

Western and non-Western history shows, instead, is two quite different lessons. One is that trends toward peace can be reversed, as Pinker's own quick sketch of human history demonstrates many times over. Periods of peace and prosperity in China were broken by times of catastrophic civil wars. The fact that the ideas of Confucius and others survived, and that their good principles were again put into action, did not prevent those blood baths from occurring. We have no reason to believe that the good and progressive ideas of the Enlightenment will protect anyone from disaster. In fact we have every reason to acknowledge the weakness of those ideas, because they failed to prevent the various totalitarian Communist experiments of the twentieth century and the equally terrible fascist experiments of the twentieth century. Karl Raimund Popper's great book, *The Open Society and Its Enemies*, explains in depth how totalitarian ideas that are part of the Western tradition, beginning with Plato, flourished in the nineteenth century and helped to bring about the Holocausts of the twentieth century.

John Howard and Count Beccaria in the eighteenth century fought to end judicial torture and imprisonment for debt—important victories of the Enlightenment that have in many cases been lost as nations have again resorted to torture in many settings. The recent record of the United States, with its practice of waterboarding and other torture, is not encouraging. The progressive Quaker idea of monastic versions of prisons also led to solitary confinement and to hideous experiments such as the Walnut Street Prison in Philadelphia in the nineteenth century and arguably to the equally horrific super-maximum security prisons of the United States, where sensory deprivation is a routine part of daily existence.

Pinker's concluding thoughts offer little reason for celebration. Poverty and violence are related, he says, and societies in which women are treated better tend to have less violence (676,686). A surplus of men tends to lead to more violence (682), and in many nations there are too many young males (688). Among the nations with current surpluses of men due to gynecide he lists Afghanistan, China, Bangladesh, Pakistan, and parts of India. Counting just half of India's population and using 2016 figures, that would mean there are too many males, and hence high motivation for violence, in areas with a total population of about 2.4 billion people, or about a third of the world's population. Pinker neglects to mention other nations that have an excess of males, which include almost all of the Muslim world and nearby sections of North and West Africa. If Pinker is correct that this imbalance of males tends toward more violence, the areas affected contain more than half of the world's people.

Most relevant to the argument of this book, Pinker maintains that there is no good evidence that advances in weaponry have a strong correlation to increases in the numbers of deaths (673), although cases like that of the Karamojong people put the lie to his thesis. Putting down traditional spears and picking up automatic rifles has made a huge difference in the numbers of deaths. He notes that while no one can claim that automatic weapons have been a good addition to the world, people tend to develop the weapons they need as situations arise and to let them rust when they are no longer needed (673–4). If nations created new weapons on demand, as many were developed and built in World War II, then there would not be such a large weapons market in the world and such close ties between national economies and the production, marketing, sales, and donation of lethal weapons. As for whether more technologically advanced weapons, such as the atomic bomb, have led to more or less casualties, that debate is moot. Some argue that an invasion of Japan by ground troops would have been far worse; some argue that the bomb was not necessary at all. Pinker does not argue, however, that there is no correlation between the availability of weapons and the number of deaths in the world.

Quantitative comparisons of deaths are offensive because human beings are not grains of sand. Whether the value of an individual life is infinite or merely very great because each of us embodies a distinctive and arguably unique take on the cosmos in which we live, it is not possible to compare lives or to assign them accurate relative values. Whatever Pinker may or may not have shown about possible reductions in the percentages of people who die in wars since ancient times, the number of current wars and the annual number of deaths due to wars is enormous. The world's economy is built to a significant degree around the continued invention, manufacture, sale, and proliferation of weapons. Of the other forces that lead to war, according to Pinker—such as poverty, gynecide, and a surplus of males in many nations—none of these are forces that are going away, and in fact if the global environment changes significantly, there is every reason to believe the force of poverty will become far greater.

There is no good reason to believe that violence is going away. There are many reasons to believe that our governments have too much invested in the preparation for violence by means of the manufacture, sales, and dissemination of weapons. The weapons market is too large a part of the world economy for violence to wane.

9

Conclusion
Cain's Crime

Our species is murderous. The worldwide culture of violence we have created may be changed in many ways. The focus of this little book has been on the seeding of the Earth with weapons, primarily small weapons, and the ways that the manufacture, marketing, and economics of weapons are woven into the structures of the world so that powers that appear to be benign and helpful are in fact to a meaningful extent built on economies of violence. Democracies are warped by the influence of the military-industrial complex.

The scope of this inquiry has been limited for the most part to small weapons, though the budgetary figures quoted have been for all forms of weapons. Little attention has been given to biological, chemical, nuclear, cyber, or other highly technical weapons whose maintenance is often beyond the abilities of small and emerging nations. In 2008, 75% of legitimate weapons sales were to developing states (Caldwell, 148), that is, to states that were in need of stability, education, health care, economic growth, infrastructure, and other basics.

Caldwell and Williams define terrorism as chiefly actions taken against noncombatants (86). Moreover, they argue that "terrorism is a strategy of the weak" (96). But terrorism is also a strategy of the strong. When the local newspaper includes a supplement that markets useless, small pieces of armor to parents, so that their children can use their backpacks as shields, that advertising is a form of terrorism. When a weapons merchant markets fighter jets and machine guns to states, pointing out what neighboring states have purchased, that is a form of sales by fear. It is terrorism. Terrorism is not merely a strategy of weaker groups like ISIS that want to punish the West for perceived wrongs. Terrorism is what any corporation does when it says that a buyer may be destroyed if the buyer does not purchase the latest upgrade of whatever weapon is under discussion. The world, in other words, has not achieved one of Franklin Roosevelt's four freedoms, the freedom from fear.

For the fiscal year 2017, the United States government planned to spend $34 billion on foreign assistance. The Peace and Security budget is $8.3 billion, or about 25% of the foreign aid. A close examination of that budget shows that much of it will be spent on weapons and on contracts and subcontracts with various private corporations that provide military services. In the same year, $4.7 billion was to be spent on educational assistance and economic development, or about 14% of the total. Health care and humanitarian aid total $16.3 billion. During 2014, the amount spent on military aid was $10.6 billion, or 25%; the amount spent on other economic assistance was $32.5 billion. The total amount of foreign assistance has declined, at least so far as the most recent budget plan can be trusted, though the percentages have remained about the same. Given the damage that weapons do, that they can be documented to cost, it seems reasonable to ask whether a change in spending priorities might make a difference in the developing world.

In 1946, Jomo Kenyatta, the revolutionary leader and first president of free Kenya, wrote his master's thesis under the direction of the great anthropologist Bronislaw Malinowski. At the end of his book, later published as *Facing Mount Kenya*, he wrote about the priorities of the colonial powers. What he said then is powerful today.

> If Africans were left in peace on their own lands, Europeans would have to offer them the benefits of white civilization in real earnest before they could obtain the African labour which they want so much. . . . They would have to let the African choose whatever parts of European culture could be adapted. He would probably not choose the gas bomb or the armed police force, but he might ask for some other things of which he does not get so much to-day. (305–6)

The United Nations World Happiness report for 2013 places Switzerland and the Scandinavian nations at the top of this scale. The United States

Conclusion

ranks 17th and Mexico 16th. Oman ranks 23rd, which is extraordinary for a nation that forty some years ago had almost no public services. The Democratic Republic of the Congo ranks 117 out of 156 nations surveyed. Iraq is 105 and Afghanistan 143. It does not seem that military interventions or the provision of weapons improve happiness, whose measurement encompasses indices of freedom and safety.

President Eisenhower's fears about the military-industrial complex lie at the root of this problem. If something walks like a duck, squawks like a duck, and swims like a duck, is it a duck? If the American national economy is built to a significant degree around the manufacture and sales of weapons to nations, if many of the world's leading powers are engaged in the same economic and political activity that involves disseminating weapons across the Earth, and if most of the members of the United Nations Security Council are simultaneously either at war or making money off preparing for war, then can it be said that the world's political and economic system is designed to produce death by war? The *reasonable* answer of course is that these same nations invest heavily in peace, healthcare, economic development, and other genuinely good projects. It therefore follows that there is no malign intent on anyone's part to proliferate warfare and the killing of soldiers and civilians. Yet the data indicate—so many data indicate—that the system in fact is built to kill. Maybe all the death is an unintended consequence of the need to defend ourselves. Maybe all the death is due to a lack of attention to the consequences of what nations do as a result of carrying out or trying to implement tens of thousands of disparate programs, visions, and agendas.

Karl Popper, the philosopher of science, argued that science advances by falsifying bad hypotheses. Usually, bad theories are abandoned, though sometimes they are put on the shelf because they contain some useful ideas. Is it possible that it is time to consider whether the idea of adding more weapons to the world has not worked as a method of gaining security?

At the end of January 2015, the top religious leader of Iran, who is no friend to the West, asked young people in the West to study Islam, anything at all about Islam. Education, he said, might help to bring an end to hostilities and violence. Those of us in Seattle involved in an effort to work with the government of Iran on cancer care, nutrition, and other issues, have found it reasonably easy to enter into discussions and to carry out initial visits and project. Alternatives to hostility are not merely possible, they are not necessarily difficult. It may be true, as the Republican candidate for president in 2016 has argued, that Iran has a holiday dedicated to hatred of America. It is certainly true that the same candidate, who now is the president, has proposed banning Muslims from entering the United States. One does not expect all hostility to end immediately. One can but try, enter into discussions, and do something constructive in the hope that a pattern of constructive activities will follow.

The Ayatollah was asking for his side of the issues to be heard, at least at the basic level of understanding some of the values that divide Islamic civilization from the West. Listening to others is critical. However, it is also true that if dialogue is limited to hearing each other's tales of woe, including stories about past wrongs, then listening is not enough. By perpetuating killing, we perpetuate more tales of woe and revenge, and those tales often incite more violence.

Romain Rolland, who won the Nobel Prize for literature shortly after World War I began for a small collection of essays, asked a very simple question that is supremely relevant today in the face of growing animosity and mutual misunderstanding, especially between the cultures of the (formerly?) Christian West and the Muslim world, or at least those significant portions of the Muslim world that feel themselves invaded physically, spiritually, intellectually, technologically, economically, morally, and in every other way. Rolland wanted the Germans and the French to ask themselves and each other what they really wanted and to try to find a way to avoid violence. Before the war end even more so during the war it appeared to be impossible to find groups willing to pose these questions. Julian Benda raised the same questions in his *Betrayal of the Intellectuals* (*La trahaison des clercs*) before World War II: why was it that those who were committed to the working of thinking about the future and about solutions to common problems had become nearly unanimous supporters of war? An answer posed in World War I by Siegfried Sassoon and other soldiers and civilians who protested was that war was profitable for those who ran industries and manufactured weapons (Graves).

Are the world's democracies sufficiently free to overcome the lobbying of the military-industrial complex to take decisive action to reduce the availability of weapons and move toward problem-solving strategies and programs that do not involve a nearly instantaneous choice to use violence? Abraham Lincoln's Annual Message to Congress on December 1, 1862, included the phrase: "We must disenthrall ourselves, and then we will

Conclusion

save our country." We are enslaved, enthralled, by our addiction to seeding weapons across the earth.

Swarthmore College, founded as a Quaker institution, maintains a website on the history of Conscientious Objection in America. During the Vietnam War, approximately 2.4 million American soldiers served in Vietnam. Of those, 58,220 died. Three million Vietnamese died. In the same period, 170,000 Americans were granted status as Conscientious Objectors. Another 300,000 were denied that status. Two hundred thousand were criminally charged. Six hundred thousand evaded the draft in various ways, including marriage. Up to 50,000 draft-age people moved to Canada. Twenty thousand moved to other nations. That is a public resistance of 1.34 million male individuals. For every 100 young men who went to Vietnam, about 56 refused or made a significant, personal, public, and sometimes costly protest. Those numbers do not begin to count the large numbers of women, of parents and grandparents, of veterans and others who also raised their voices in anguish at what the United States was doing to itself as well as to those in other nations.

These numbers are easier to find than a total of the number of people who worked in the Civil Rights movement, or who are currently active in the Black Lives Matter movement. The point of the example is that there can be no doubt that if enough people express concern about violence, and specifically about the manufacture and sales of weapons, that public witness may begin to change the deeply embedded American and worldwide political and economic structure that is based on the production of weapons and the export of violence. Priorities may begin to change toward economic development, health care, education, and other goods. Many of the examples in this book have been drawn from the United States because the author is a citizen of that nation. The United States, however, is also the primary manufacturer and marketer of weapons. While there have been successful anti-war efforts in the United States that continue now with movements such as Black Lives Matter, it is also true that such movements have had major impacts throughout the world. The names of Mohandas Gandhi, Nelson Mandela, and Giovanni Lanza del Vasto come to mind as well as Tolstoy's pacifist masterpiece, *The Kingdom of God is Within You*. Many of those who advocate for nonviolent solutions are nameless, such as the thousands of people who stood silently in Tiananmen Square or those who stood in the neighborhoods of Manila between the presidential palace and the military barracks at the end of the Ferdinand Marcos regime. Quite contrary to the voices of militarists, the way of peaceful change has often been effective and can continue to be so.

The difficulty that witnesses to peace face is one of mind over matter. Violence has the ability to focus attention very narrowly. Violence promises quick solutions. Problems are defined in terms of short-term victory over an immediate threat. Every form of peacemaking requires a slow process of education, witnessing, mourning, and actions that involve still more witnessing and education. There are of course many ways that peace can be increased, and the efforts of those who negotiate treaties and covenants are not negligible. The main points of this book are that the level of violence is extraordinary, that the availability of small and large arms is a major part of the problem that must be addressed, and that availability of weapons is due in a significant degree to economic motivations to make and sell weapons, even though the evidence is clear that the use of weapons produces damage far beyond the sales value of those weapons and prevents progress on issues that are widely agreed to be important: the environment, health, poverty, starvation, and education, among many others.

Life is valuable. More valuable than we generally think.

Swords can be beaten into ploughshares. It will take planning and thought, however, to turn political and economic systems that are dedicated to the perpetuation of violence to change into systems that find their power and satisfaction and success in producing education, health care, global sustainability, and other goods on which we may come to agree. As Romain Rolland asked a century ago: What exactly is it that people want? Could the nations in conflict ask themselves what they are attempting to achieve for themselves and for others? Is it possible, moreover, to establish governments that are more democratic in the sense that they are more dedicated to identifying and resolving issues through debate and deliberation, and through the collection and testing of data, rather than by defaulting to violent solutions that produce more conflict?

Until then, the civilization in which we live, and above all the civilization of the advanced industrial countries, is a civilization dedicated to committing Cain's crime.

Bibliography

Abbott, Martin, Karen Smith, and Thomas Trzyna. *Winning the Math Wars: No Teacher Left Behind*. Seattle: University of Washington Press, 2008.
"Academic Ranking of World Universities." www.shanghairanking.com.
"Afghanistan Civilian Casualties." http://www.theguardian.com/news/datablog/2010/aug/10/afghanistan-civilian-casualties-statistics.
Afghanistan Civilian Casualties. https://en.wikipedia.org/wiki/Civilian_casualties_in_the_war_in_Afghanistan_(2001–present).
Agentorangerecord.com. http://www.agentorangerecord.com/home.
Alexander, Michelle. *The New Jim Crow: Mass Incarceration in the Age of Colorblindness*. New York: The New Press, 2014.
Anuak people. https://en.wikipedia.org/wiki/Anuak_people.
Arendt, Hannah. *The Human Condition*. Chicago: University of Chicago Press, 1958.
"Arms Industry Ramps Up Lobbying." https://www.opensecrets.org/influence.
Bauder, Jeremy. "15 of the Most Expensive Projects Abandoned by the US Military." *Business Insider*, January 29, 2016. http://www.businessinsider.com/some-of-the-militarys-most-expensive-sunk-cost-projects-2016-1.
Beccaria, Cesare. *On Crimes and Punishments*. Translated by Henry Paolucci. New York: MacMillan, 1988.
Belkaid, Akram. "L'école algérienne face au piege identitaire." *Le Monde Diplomatique*, August 2016, 6–7.
Bellah, Robert. "American Civil Religion." *Journal of the American Academy of Arts and Sciences* 96 (Winter 1967) 1–21.
Belvedere, Matthew J. "Trump asks why US can't use nukes: MSNBC." *CNBC*, August 3, 2016. https://www.cnbc.com/2016/08/03/trump-asks-why-us-cant-use-nukes-msnbcs-joe-scarborough-reports.html.
Benda, Julien. *La trahaison des clercs*. Paris: Grasset, 1975.
Bentham, Jeremy. *Panopticon*. London: Verso, 1995.
Berman, Mark. "Even more blacks were lynched in the U.S. than previously though, study finds." *Washington Post*, February 10, 2015, Post Nation. http://www.washingtonpost.com/even-more-black-people-were-lynched-in-the-us.
Bernish, Claire. "So It begins: American Police Start Pushing to Weaponize Domestic Drones." Anti Media, March 20, 2016. http://theantimedia.com/american-police-start-pushing-to-weaponize-domestic-drones/.

Bibliography

Bertrand, Natasha. "Congress quietly renewed a ban on gun-violence research." *Business Insider*, July 7, 2015. http://www.businessinsider.com/congress-ban-on-gun-violence-research-renewed.

Brady Campaign to Prevent Gun Violence. www.bradycampaign.org.

Breslow, Jason M. "The Staggering Toll of Mexico's Drug War." *Frontline*, July 27, 2015, Drug Lord: The Legend of Shorty. http://www.pbs.org/wgbh/frontline/article/the-staggering-toll-of-mexicos-drug-war.

Bureau of Labor Statistics. "US Employment Tables by Sector." http://www.bls.gov.emp.ep_table_201.html.

Caldwell, Dan, and Robert E. Williams, Jr. *Seeking Security in an Insecure World*. 2nd ed. New York: Rowman and Littlefield, 2012.

Center for World University Rankings, The. http://www.CWUR.org.

Chadwick, Lauren, and R. Jeffrey Smith. "Congress Buys the Navy a $400 Million Pork Ship." *Politico Magazine*, July 5, 2016, War Room. https://www.politico.com/magazine/story/2016/07/littoral-combat-ship-congress-navy-pentagon-400-million-pork-214009.

Chen, Siyan, Norman V. Loayza, and Marta Reynal-Querol. "The Aftermath of Civil War." World Bank, April 2007, Post-Conflict Transitions Working Paper No. 4. https://openknowledge.worldbank.org/handle/10986/7006.

Chomsky, Noam. *Failed States: The Abuse of Power and the Assault on Democracy*. London: Penguin, 2006.

ClearedConnections.com. "Defense Jobs Make up 10 Percent of U.S. Manufacturing Demand." https://www.clearedconnections.com/security-clearance-news/security-clearance/defense-jobs-make-up-10-percent-of-u-s-manufacturing-demand.htm.

Cohen, Alexander. "Defense Contractors Spend Millions to Undo Military Budget Caps." http://www.time.com/3984453/defense-contractor-lobbying.

Collier, Paul. "Development and Conflict." http://www.un.org/esa/documents/Development.and.Conflict2.pdf.

Collier, Paul, et al. "Beyond Greed and Grievance: Feasibility and Civil War." Department of Economics, Oxford University. http://www.oep.oxfordjournals.org/content/6/1/1.

Collins, Ross. "Gun Control and the Old West." https://www.ndsu/pubweb/~rcollins/scholarship/guns.html.

Conrad, Joseph. *Heart of Darkness*. In *The Conrad Argosy*. New York: Doubleday, 1942.

Conroy, Bill. "Drug War-Related Homicides In The US Average At Least 1,100 a Year." https://narcosphere.narconews.com/notebook/bill-conroy/2012/03/drug-war-related-homicides-us-average-least-1100-year.

"Contemporary Slavery." https://www.wikipedia.org/wiki/Contemporary-slavery.

Crime Prevention Research Center. "Comparing Murder Rates and Gun Ownership Across Nations." Crimeresearch.org/2014/03/comparing-murder-rates-across-countries.

De las Casas, Bartolomé. *An Account Much Abbreviated of the Destruction of the Indies*. Translated by Andrew Hurley. Cambridge: Hackett, 2003.

Deghan, Saeed, and Richard Norton-Taylor. "Sales of Weapons to Gulf States up 70% over Five Years." https://www.theguardian.com>world>arms-trade.

"Department of Defense Revolving Door in Full Swing." www.politico.com/. . ./department-of-defense-revolving-door-in-full-swing-098813.

Diamond, Jared. *Guns, Germs and Steel*. New York: Norton, 2017. "Do People Really buy Weapons from Dark Web Markets?" https://www.deepdotweb.com>featured.

Bibliography

Downes, Alexander B. *Targeting Civilians in War*. Ithaca: Cornell University Press, 2008.

Duke, Christopher. Conditions in Venezuela. Personal communications. September 2105, July 2016.

Eisenhower, Dwight D. "Farewell Address, January 17, 1961." https://www.wikipedia.org/wiki/Eisenhower%27s_farewell_address.

Eremenko, Alexey. "Russia's classified Ukraine crisis death toll." www.nbcnews.com/.../ukraine-crisis/russias-classified-ukraine-death-toll-appears.

EulerHermes.com. "Oman Current Account Deficit." www.eulerhermes.com>Euler Hermes>Economic research>Country Reports.

Fagan, Jeffrey. *Gangs in America*. Thousand Oaks, California: Sage, 1996.

Faridzadeh, Mehdi. Personal communication, September 2015.

———. *Philosophies of Just War in Greek Philosophy and Religions of Abraham: Judaism, Christianity, and Islam*. New York: Global Scholarly, 2004.

Fisher, Julian Monroe. "The Explorer's Club Flag Expedition #89 Report: 2010 Congo Expedition to Katanga." www.julianmonroefisher.com/pages/.../Julian%Fisher_flag_report_2010.pdf.

ForeignAssistance.gov. Accessed 7/9/16.

Gardam, Judith. *Necessity, Proportionality and the Use of Force by States*. Cambridge: Cambridge University Press, 2004.

———. *Non-Combatant Immunity as a Norm of International Humanitarian Law*. London: Nijhoff, 1993.

Geneva Declaration on Armed Violence and Development. "Global Burden of Armed Violence 2015: Every Body Counts." www.genevadeclaration.org/.../global-burden-of-armed-violence.

George W. Bush Foreign Affairs. https://www.millercenter.org/president/gwbush/foreignaffairs.

Gibbon, Edward. *The Decline and Fall of the Roman Empire*. New York: Dent, 1969.

Gil-Alana, Luis A., and Prakrash Singh. "Economic Growth and Recovery After Civil Wars." Econpapers.repec.org/REPEC:bpj:pepspp:v:20:y:2014.

GlobalFirePower.com. www.GlobalFirePower.com.

GlobalRiskInsights.com. "Sultan Qaboos and the Omani Economy." www.globalriskinsights.com/.../power-broker-series-sultan-qaboos-and-the-omani-economy.

Graves, Robert. *Goodbye to All That*. New York: Vintage, 1958.

Gray, John. "Steven Pinker is wrong about violence and war." https://theguardian.com/Arts>Books>Society.

Green, Victor. *The Negro Motorist Green Book*. New York: Victor Green, 1940.

GulfBase.com. "Oman Petroleum Income." www.gulfbase.com/Gcc/Index/5.

GulfBusiness.com. "Oman Aims to Cut Expat Bosses." www.gulfbusiness.com/oman-cut-expat-bosses-oil-austerity-hits/.

"Gunfight at the OK Corral." https://en.wikipedia.org/wiki/gunfight-at-the-ok-corral.

Haber, Joram Graf, ed. *Absolutism and Its Consequentialist Critics*. Lanham, Maryland: Rowman and Littlefield, 1994.

"Hammarskjold Brands Baluba Slaughter as Act of Genocide. Milwaukee Sentinel. 9/1/60." www.jsonline.com.

Hartung, William D. "Corporate Welfare for Weapons Makers." http://www.cato.org/.../corporate-welfare-weaons-makers.

Bibliography

Hines, Lindsay, et al. "Are the Armed Forces Understood and Supported by the Public? Armed Forces and Society." https://www/kcl.ac.uk/kcmhr/publications/assetfiles/2014/Hines2014.pdf.
"Honduras Profile." www.insightcrime.org/honduras-organized-crime-news/honduras.
"Honduras Set to Lose Title." www.insightcrime.org/honduras-set-to-lose-title.
Houellebecq, Michel. *Soumission*. Paris: Flammarion, 2015.
"How to Waste $100 Billion." www.forbes.com/sites/.../12/.../how-to-waste-100-billion.
Howard, John. *The State of the Prisons*. New York: Gale, 2010.
Inspector General. "Report on Weapons Lost in Afghanistan." www.freebeacon.com/.../report-420m-in-u-s-weapons.
Institutional Animal Care and Use Committee Guidebook. Office of Laboratory Animal Welfare. Applied Research Ethics National Association. 2nd Edition, 2002, Reprinted 2008.
International Coalition for the Responsibility to Protect. www.responsibilitytoprotect.
International Committee of the Red Cross. San Remo Manual. www.ICRC.com.
International Physicians for the Prevention of Nuclear War. "Health Effects of Uranium Mining." www.ippnw.org/ican/uranium-mining.html.
Iraq Body Count Project. https://en.wikipedia.org/wiki/Iraq_Body_Count_project.
Jabs, Lorelle. Personal communication. Karamajong people. September, 2013.
"The Jungle Gangs of Jharkhand." www.hindustantimes.com/static/the-jungle-gangs-of-jharkand.
Kakutani, Michiko. "King Leopold's Ghost: Genocide with Spin Control." www.nytimes.com/books/98/08/30/daily/leopold-book-review.html.
Kellermann, Arthur L. and Frederick P. Rivara. "Silencing the Science on Gun Research." www.jama.jamanetwork.com/journals/fullarticle/1487470.
Kenyatta, Jomo. *Facing Mount Kenya*. New York: Vintage, 1962.
Khamenei, Ayatollah Ali. "Iran's Supreme Leader Pens Open Letter to the Young People of the West." www.cnn.com/2015/1/22/middleeast/iran-ayatollah-letter/index.html.
Kleinman, Avery. "Revolving Door." www.otherwords.org/partners/project-on-government-oversight.
Kohlberg, Lawrence. *Essays on Moral Development*. San Francisco: Harper Row, 1981.
Kroeber, Theodora. *Ishi in Two Worlds*. Berkeley: University of California, 1960.
Kutty, Samuel. "Fear of Job Loss Grips Expats." www.2016.omanobserver/fear-of-job-loss-grips-expats.
"Kwangju Uprising." https://www.britannica.com/events/kwangju-uprising.
Le Clézio, Jean-Marie Gustave. *Désert*. Paris: Gallimard, 1980.
———. *Révolutions*. Paris: Gallimard, 2003.
"Lead and the shooting range." www.thewellarmedwoman.com/media/videos/twaw-today/lead-on-the-range.
Levi-Strauss, Claude. *Tristes Tropiques*. Paris: Plon, 1955.
"License to Carry." https://www.dps.texas/rsd/chl.
Lincoln, Abraham. "Annual Message to Congress, 12/1/1862." www.abrahamlincoln.org/lincoln/speeches/congress.html.
"List of countries by firearm related death rate." https://en.wikipedia.org/wiki/list-of-countries-by-firearm-related-death-rate.
"List of ongoing armed conflicts." https://en.wikipedia.org/wiki/list-of-ongoing-armed-conflicts.

Bibliography

"List of ongoing protests and civil unrest." https://en.wikipedia.org/wiki/list-of-ongoing-protests-and-civil-unrest.

Littell, Jonathan. *Les Bienviellantes*. Paris: Gallimard, 2006.

"Loaded with lead: How gun ranges poison workers and shooters." *Seattle Times*. Projects. seattletimes.com/2014/loaded-with-lead/4/

Lorenz, Konrad. *On Aggression*. New York: Harvest, 1974.

Lykketoft, Mogens. "Letter to All Permanent Representatives, July 21, 2016." www.un.org/apps/news/story.asp?NEWSID=54522.

Majumdar, Dave. "Four Future US Weapons of War that Should be Canceled Now." Nationalinterest.org/feature/4-future-us-weapons-that-should-be-canceled-now.

"Mauritania." *Human Rights Watch World Report 1989*. https://www.hrw.org.reports/1989/WR89.

Merton, Thomas. *Ishi Means Man: Essays on Native Americans*. Greensboro, North Carolina: Unicorn, 1976.

"Mexico's 1968 Massacre: What Really Happened?" NPR, December 1, 2008, All Things Considered, produced by Joe Richman and Anayasi Diaz-Cortes. https://www.npr.org/templates/story/story.php?storyId=97546687.

Military.com. "Panama." www.military.com/Resources/History/SubmittedFileView?file=history_panama.html.

Mill, John Stuart. *On Liberty*. London: Penguin, 1985.

Mo Tzu. *Basic Writings*. Translated by Burton Watson. New York: Columbia University, 1963.

Moore, G. E. *Principia Ethica*. Cambridge: Cambridge University Press, 1959.

Morris, James. *Sultan in Oman*. New York: Pantheon, 1957.

Nerad, Maresi, Mimi Heggelund, and Thomas Trzyna, *Toward a Global Ph.D.: Forces and Forms of Doctoral Education Worldwide*. Seattle: University of Washington Press, 2010.

"National Rifle Association: Lobbying." https://www.opensecrets.org/lobby/clientsum.php?id=d000000082.

Nehlen, Paul. "Deport All Muslims." www.thedailybeast.com/. . ./paul-nehlen-paul-ryans-challenger-deport-all-muslims.html.

Numbeo.com. "World Crime and Safety Index, Mid-Year 2016." https://www.numbeo.crime>indexbycity>worldmap.

O'Connor, Anne-Marie, and William Booth. "Mexican Drug Cartels Targeting and Killing Children." Washington Post, April 9, 2011, World. https://www.washingtonpost.com/world/mexican-drug-cartels-targeting-and-killing-children/2011/04/07/AFwkFb9C_story.html?utm_term=.fbea4e0084ad.

Office of the Special Adviser on the Prevention of Genocide. www.un.org/en/genocideprevention.

"Pharmaceuticals/Health Products Lobbying." https://www.opensecrets.org/industries/indus.php?ind=H04.

Piketty, Thomas. *Capital in the Twenty-First Century*. Cambridge: Harvard University Press, 2014.

Popper, Karl. *The Open Society and Its Enemies*. New Haven: Princeton, 1946.

Popper-Lynkeus, Joseph. *The Individual and the Value of Human Life*. Translated by Andrew Kirk Kelley with Joram Graf Haber. Lanham, Maryland: Rowman and Littlefield, 1995.

Bibliography

"Program for International Student Assessment, 2012 Scores." https://www.oecd.org/pisa/keyfindings/pisa-2012-results-overview.pdf.
Public Health Service Policy on Humane Care and Use of Laboratory Animals. Office of Laboratory Animal Welfare. National Institutes of Health, 2002.
Qiu, Linda. "Emma Watson: More lives are lost due to gender discrimination than in all 20th century wars." www.politifact.com/global.../emma-watson-more-lives-are-lot-due-to-gender-discrimination.
Rawls, John. *A Theory of Justice, Revised Edition.* Cambridge: Harvard University Press, 1999.
Reidhead, SJ. "The Myth of Guns and the Wild West." http://www.thepinkflamingoblog.com/2017/10/23/the-myth-of-guns-and-the-libertarian-wild-west/.
"The Responsibility to Protect." www.responsibilitytoprotect.org.
"Responsibility to Protect." https://en.wikipedia/wiki/Responsibility-to-protect.
"Revolving Door." https:"www.opensecrets.org/revolving.
Robarge, David. "CIA's Covert Operations in the Congo, 1960–68." https://www.cia.gov/...Robarge-FRUS.
Rodriguez. Stephen. "Top 10 Failed Defense Programs of the RMA Era." https://warontherocks.com/2014/12/top-10-failed-defense-programs-of-the-rma-era.
Rolland, Romain. *Au-dessus de la melee.* Paris: Payot, 2013.
RT Question More. "US, Papua New Guinea and Oman are Only Nations without Paid Maternity Leave." https://www.rt.com/usa/158776.
Russell, Bertrand. *Why I am Not a Christian.* New York: Simon and Schuster, 1957.
"Sales of US Arms Fuels the Wars of Arab States." *New York Times.* https://www.nytimes.com/2015/04/.../sales-of-us-arms-fuels-the-wars-of-arab-states.
"San Remo Manual." Ihl-databses.icrc.org/ihl/INTRO/560?OpenDocument.
Sansal, Boualem. *2084.* Paris: Gallimard, 2015.
———. *Dis-moi le paradis.* Paris: Gallimard, 2003.
———. *Poste Restante, Alger.* Paris: Gallimard, 2006.
Scaruffi, Pietro. "Wars and Casualties of the 20th and 21st Centuries." www.scaruffi.com/politics/massacres.html.
Sen, Amartya. "More Than 100 Million Women are Missing." www.nybooks.com/articles/1990/12/20/more-than-100-million-women-are-missing.
Serres, Michel. *La Guerre mondiale.* Paris: Le Pommier, 2008.
Shadman, Mazyar. Personal communication, Fred Hutchinson Cancer Research Center, September 2015.
"Small Arms Survey 2015." www.smallarmssurvey.org.
"Small Arms: No Single Solution: UN Chronicle." www.smallarmssurvey.org.
Stanton, Gregory. "Countries at Risk, 2012." www.genocidewatch.org/images/countries-at-risk-2012-report.pdf.
"Stopbulletsnow.com." Seattle Times supplement, June 7, 2016. www.stopbulletsnow.com.
"Strategies for Reducing Gun Violence (2007)." Public Safety Canada. www.publicsafety.gc.ca/cnt/rsrcs/pblctns/rdcng-gn-vlnc.
"Stubborn Facts." www.theblazecom/.../nr-draft-how-important-are-guns-to-the-u-s-economy.
Sullivan, Paul. "Can Saudi Arabia Vision 2030 Get the Kingdom Off the Oil-Economy Roller Coaster." National Council on US Arab Relations. https://ncusar.org/aa/.../can-vision-2030-get-kingdom-off-oil-economy-roller-coaster.
"Summary of the Responsibility to Protect." www.responsibilitytoprotect.org.

Bibliography

"Terrorism and Other Harms of Believing in an Afterlife." www.humanismbyJoe.co/terrorism-and-other-harms-of-believing-in-an-afterlife.

Thomas, Richard. "Maths scores in Oman among the weakest in the world." www.MuscatDaily.com/. . ./oman/maths-scores-in-oman-among-the-weakest-in-the-world.

Thompson, Mark. "Costly Flight Hours." *Time*, April 2, 2013. http://nation.time.com/2013/04/02/costly-flight-hours/.

"Tlateco Massacre." www.npr.org/templates/story/story.php?storyid=97546687.

Tolstoy, Leo. *The Kingdom of God is Within You*. New York: Dover, 2006.

———. *War and Peace*. Translated by Ann Dunnigan. London: Penguin 1968. "Top Industries in Lobbying." https://www.statista.com/industries>society>politics&government.

"Top Spenders." https://www.opensecrets.org/lobby/top.

Trzyna, Thaddeus. Personal communications, 2015–16.

Trzyna, Thomas. *Blessed are the Pacifists: The Beatitudes and Just War Theory*. Scottsdale, PA: Herald, 2006.

———. "The Eumenides," in *Karl Popper and Literary Theory: Critical Rationalism as a Philosophy of Literature*. Leiden: Brill, 2016, (139–66).

———. *Le Clézio's Spiritual Quest*. Berlin: Lang, 2012.

———. *Forgiveness: A Review of a Moral Conflict in Eighteenth Century English Thought, with studies of Fielding, Goldsmith, Richardson and Rowe*. Diss. University of Washington, 1977.

"Twentieth Century Atlas–Worldwide Statistics of Casualties." www.necrometrics.com/all20c.html.

United Nations Charter. Article 97. www.un.org.

UN Chronicle. "Small Arms: No Single Solution." https://unchronicle.un.org/article/small-arms-no-single-solution.

"UN to Probe Whether Iconic Secretary General was Assassinated." Foreignpolicy.com/. . ./u-n-to-probe-whether-iconic-secretary-general-was-assassinated.

United Nations Development Program. "Post Conflict Economic Recovery, Crisis Prevention and Recovery Report, 2008." www.undp.org/. . ./crisis-prevention-and-recovery-report-2008.

U.S. Department of State. "US Relations with Oman." https://www.state.gov/r/pa/ei/bgn/35834.html.

"US Still #1 at Selling Arms to the World." Time.com/4161613/us-arms-sales-exports-weapons.

"US Weapons Jobs, 2012." www.siteselection.com.

VandenDolder, Tess. "Why Everyone is Lobbying on the F35 Jet." Dcinno.streetwise.co/2014/10/09/why-everyone-is-lobbying-on-the-f35-jet.

Velez, Erin Dunlop. "America's College Drop Out Epidemic." Working Paper, Calder Center, January 2014. https://caldercenter.org/sites/default/files/WP-109-Final.pdf.

Victor, Philip. "Amnesty International says Rohingya death toll higher than UN estimates." America.aljazeera.com/articles/2015/amnesty-report.

Walzer, Michael. *Arguing about War*. New Haven: Yale, 2004.

Wang, Amie, et al. "Adult Attitudes Toward the Military: Poll One." Defense Manpower Data Center.U.S. Department of Defense. http:www.dtic.mil/cgi-bin/GetTRDoc?AD=ADA41646.

Bibliography

Watson, Emma. "More Lives are Lost Due to Gender Discrimination than in all 20th Century Wars." Sheddingtheego.com/.../emma-watson-more-lives.are-lost-due-to-gender-discrimination.

Weil, Simone. *Oeuvres*. Paris: Gallimard, 1999.

"Where did Iran get its military arms over the last 70 years?" https://www.pri.org/stories/.../where-did-iran-get-its-military-arms-over-the-last-70-years.

"White House Acknowledges up to 166 Civilian Deaths in Counter-Terror Strikes." www.politico.com/story/2016/07/civilian-deaths-counterterror-drone-strikes-225038.

Whiteman, Hilary. "India heat wave kills 2330 people." www.cnn.com/2015/06/01/asia/india-heat-wave-deaths.

Williams, Susan. *Spies in the Congo*. London: Hurst, 2016.

———. *Who Killed Hammarskjold?* Oxford: Oxford, 2014.

Winkler, Adam. "Did the Wild West Have More Gun Control than We do Today?" www.huffingtonpost.com/adam-winkler/did-the-wild-west-have-more-gun-control-than-we-do-today.

"Wiwa et al. vs Royal Dutch Shell et al." Center for Constitutional Justice. https://ccrjustice.org>what we do>historic cases.

Woodward, David. American Cultural Exchange. Conversations about Iran, 2015.

Worldbank.org. "Education Expenditures." www.data.worldbank/indicator/SE.XPD.TOTL.GB.ZS.

Worldbank.org. "Health Expenditures." www.data.worldbank/indicator/SH.XPD.PUB.ZS.

Worldbank.org. "Military Expenditures." www.data.worldbank/indicator/MS.MIL.XPND.GD.ZS.

Wright, Austin. "The Mighty F35 Lobby." www.politico.com/.../the-mighty-f-35-lobby.

www.ingramcontent.com/pod-product-compliance
Lightning Source LLC
Chambersburg PA
CBHW030902170426
43193CB00009BA/716